D1346264

LITERARY AND
ARTISTIC LANDMARKS
OF
EDINBURGH

Scott's House – 39 North Castle Street

LITERARY AND ARTISTIC LANDMARKS OF EDINBURGH

By

ANDREW PENNYCOOK

Foreword by

SIR COMPTON MACKENZIE

Illustrated by

EDWARD SWANN

CHARLES SKILTON

THE ALBYN PRESS

EDINBURGH

© The Albyn Press 1973

Printed by
T & A Constable Ltd
Edinburgh

Published by
THE ALBYN PRESS
3 Abbeymount
Edinburgh
and
50 Alexandra Road
London SW19

The illustrations are
based on various
sources and do
not necessarily
represent the
present-day
aspect

ILLUSTRATIONS

Scott's House – 39 North Castle Street   Frontispiece

page

Hume's Lodgings, Riddle's Close, 322 High Street   19

Smollett's House, St. John Street, Canongate   23

James's Court, 50 High Street   27

William Blackwood's Office at 45 George Street   99

Raeburn's Studio at 32 York Place   109

Carlyle's House – 21 Comely Bank   113

Stevenson's House – 17 Heriot Row   117

Blackwood's Saloon at 45 George Street   123

FOREWORD

I have read this fascinating story of the literary and artistic past of Edinburgh as enthusiastically as once upon a time I used to read the history of Athens. This book will be an invaluable guide not only to those who visit Edinburgh at Festival time but for tourists who visit it at any time. I congratulate the publisher for recognizing the quality of this book which is very much needed at the present moment when people seem to think that the historical past started in 1960.

Budding authors today will flower more profusely when they have read this entrancing book.

COMPTON MACKENZIE

Edinburgh.

PREFACE

The original inspiration for this book came from Laurence Hutton's fascinating work *Literary Landmarks of Edinburgh*, which was first published over eighty years ago. It had been intended to reprint this book as it stood but fashions have changed in the intervening period and reputations have both risen and fallen. This meant that many of the people mentioned by Hutton are no longer considered to be as important as they were then, while others were deserving of more extended treatment.

Therefore, it was decided that a new version should be written based closely on the structure adopted by Hutton, but changing the amount of space given to the various figures that appeared. But as the book progressed it gained a momentum of its own which led to the inclusion of rather more details of the way of life of Edinburgh in past centuries as well as a great many more anecdotes about the literary giants who passed under her smoky skies.

One reason for this was, undoubtedly, the fact that the passage of time has now removed us from direct contact with Edinburgh's golden age. For example, when he was standing one morning in St James's Square, trying to make out which house Burns had lived in for a time, Hutton was asked by an old man, a plasterer by profession, if he were looking for the poet's window. Naturally Hutton was curious to find out how much this stranger knew about it and learned that, in his boyhood, the plasterer had been a friend of Burns's 'Clarinda'. Nowadays, our contemporaries are too close to write about with comfort, while no one survives from Stevenson's Edinburgh days. That there are still remarkable links with the past, however, is shown for instance by a letter which appeared in the *Sunday Express* in 1968.

Fifty years before, as a schoolboy, the correspondent's brother was sitting reading in the sunshine in Dundee, outside the Victoria Art Gallery, when he was approached by an old man who asked: 'What are you reading, laddie?'

'*Waverley,*' was the reply.

'Take this shilling,' said the old man, 'and I'll tell you why.

'When I was your age I was sitting in the sunshine reading one day when an old man came up to me and asked the same question. "*Rob Roy,*" I replied.

'He handed me a shilling and explained: "When I was your age I was sitting reading in the sun one day in Princes Street Gardens in Edinburgh when an old man came up to me and said, 'What are you reading, my lad?'

'"'*Heart of Midlothian,*' I said.

'"'I wrote that book,' said the old man. 'Here is a shilling to remember me by.'"'

I hope that this will be a book to remember some of Edinburgh's former inhabitants by.

A.P.

10

Edinburgh has always been a city with literary and artistic links. Poets and critics, historians and novelists, philosophers and scientists, in all degrees of brilliance, have been born there or have been attracted by its renown. The internationally famous teachers at the University have naturally been part of the reason for this but the welcoming character of the inhabitants to creative talent has also played a considerable part. Indeed Edinburgh is exceptional for the interest taken by its populace in the writers and artists that have lived there, and this is evidenced by the number of statues and public memorials which the city possesses. As the visitor leaves Waverley Station he is greeted by the sight of the Scott monument, towering 200 feet over Princes Street—a fitting memorial to one of the city's greatest sons. But Edinburgh has statues or memorials to writers as diverse as Burns, who was a visitor, and Dugald Stewart, who was a professor of moral philosophy at the University.

In the short space of this volume there is little more that can be done than to traverse the most important part of the enormous list of famous men, from Drummond of Hawthornden to Hugh MacDiarmid, who have at some time graced the 'Athens of the North' with their presence and to try to give some picture of them as men and of the city they lived in.

William Drummond of Hawthornden, sometimes called the 'Scottish Petrarch', passed most of his life as a retired country gentleman at Hawthornden on the banks of the Esk, one of the beauty spots near the capital. It was here that Ben Jonson paid him a visit in 1618 or 1619. According to the story Drummond was sitting under a huge sycamore tree when Jonson's enormous figure came into sight, and he greeted him with the line 'Welcome! Welcome! Royal Ben!' only to receive the rhyming reply 'Thank'ee kindly Hawthornden!'

Although he spent so much of his time away from the city of

Edinburgh his links with the capital were very strong—he was educated at the High School and at the University before studying law at Bourges and Paris. The first 'Hie Schule', at which he was a pupil, was built in 1567 in the garden of the monastery of the Blackfriars, at the end of Infirmary Street and near the head of the High School Wynd. This school was demolished in 1777 to make way for the second High School (now known as the Old Infirmary and part of the University). The university buildings Drummond knew have also been built over by the present university buildings and no portion of the older structure has been preserved.

Hawthornden, described by its owner as a sweet flowery place 'far from the madding worldling's hoarse discords' is easily reached by bus from the city, and the house still remains. It is not the identical mansion which Jonson knew since it was extensively enlarged and altered by William Drummond twenty years after their encounter. Apart from his ability as a poet, Drummond is best remembered today for his use of this meeting in his book *Conversations of Ben Jonson with William Drummond.* Jonson might not have been so free with his speech (or his thanks) if he had known that his host was to become, at his expense, the inventor of interviewing.

The Scot who was to excel Drummond in this style brought another Johnson to Scotland in 1773. On the night of 14 August in that year he received the following note: 'Mr Johnson sends his compliments to Mr Boswell, being just arrived at Boyd's.' He only stayed for four days on this occasion but after their return from the Hebrides he remained for about a fortnight in the Scottish capital, as Boswell's guest.

Johnson's prejudices against Scotland, and Scotsmen, are well known, and he must have had them reinforced soon after his arrival, for on asking to have his lemonade made sweeter (he was not drinking anything alcoholic at the time), the waiter

12

'lifted a lump of sugar with his greasy fingers' and put it into the drink. The Doctor, with indignation, threw the lemonade out of the window. His attitude cannot have been improved either by his walk from Boyd's to Boswell's house. The people in the high tenements still shouted 'Gardy loo' as they hurled their slops from the windows. Indeed it was said that 'walking the streets of Edinburgh at night is pretty perilous'. The magistrates did try to enforce the city laws against throwing foul water from the windows, but the structure of the houses in the old town, consisting as they did of many storeys in each of which a different family lived, and the use of open sewers, meant that the streets were noted for their stench. As Doctor Johnson grumbled in Boswell's ear, 'I smell you in the dark!'

On this first stay Johnson was shown most of the sights of Edinburgh by Boswell and some of the other intellectual giants of the city, and greeted each one in a suitable manner. Shown the part of Holyrood palace where Queen Mary had lived and in which Rizzio was murdered, the great doctor let himself be overheard muttering a line from the old ballad *Johnnie Armstrong's Last Good-night*—'And ran him through the fair bodie'. Taken to the great church of St Giles (which was, at this time, divided into four places of worship) he remarked: 'Come, let me see what was once a church!' Inside they found it was elegantly fitted out, but shamefully dirty. Johnson said nothing but, when they came to the door of the Royal Infirmary and he saw the notice 'Clean Your Feet' he turned and slyly said: 'There is no occasion for putting this at the doors of your churches.'

Boswell later showed him an old wall, enclosing part of the university, which he remembered used to bulge out in a threatening manner, and about which there was a tradition (like the one about Bacon's study in Oxford) that it would fall upon a very learned man. The university had replaced it some

13

time before their visit to let the street be widened but Doctor Johnson suggested dryly that they were afraid it would never fall.

During his stay he met, and was entertained by, the great, the learned and the elegant and was always given the most generous hospitality. Except from Boswell's father, Lord Auchinleck, who was horrified at his son's devotion to Johnson. 'Jamie has gaen clean gyte. . . . Whae's tail do ye think he has preened himself tae noo? A dominie man—an auld dominee who keepit a schule and caa'ed it an Acaademy!' In fact, the great lexicographer pleased none of the Boswells except his four-month-old daughter Veronica. Auchinleck made many cutting remarks even after he had seen the sage: 'He's only a dominie, and the worst mannered dominie I ever met.' But Boswell's wife was not much more favourable in her opinions: 'I have often seen a bear led by a man but never till now have I seen a man led by a bear.' The eventual publication of the famous biography did not make things any better and Boswell's brothers were horribly ashamed of it, and of him.

Indeed Boswell was well known for always getting into trouble of various kinds and one day soon after his father's death, when he met the old Scots lawyer Lord Kames being helped into his sedan chair to go to Parliament House, he was hailed with 'I shall shortly be seeing your father, have you any message for him?' Boswell must have been very used to Kames' attitude towards him for on one occasion he complained to the old judge that he, Boswell, was occasionally dull. Reassuringly the reply began 'Homer sometimes nods,' only to continue cynically, 'indeed, sir, it is the only chance you have of resembling him.'

Boyd's, at which Johnson alighted on his first arrival in Edinburgh, was the White Horse Inn in Boyd's Close, St Mary's Wynd, Canongate, but tavern, close and wynd have long vanished before the broom of development. St Mary's Wynd has now been replaced by St Mary's Street and the site of the inn is marked with a tablet recording the association with Boswell and Johnson. The White Horse Inn was, in Boswell's day, one of the best hostelries in the town, and it continued as a coaching house until the close of the eighteenth century. It must not be confused, however, with the White Horse Inn that appears in *Waverley*. At the end of the nineteenth century this still stood as a picturesque ruin, with shattered gables, broken chimneys and the date 1523 faintly visible over its window, at the foot of White Horse Wynd at the other end of the Canongate. The inn has now been reconstructed, on the same site, and stands in White Horse Close. Doubtless imaginative visitors will be able to conjure up its exciting past as a resort for the officers of Prince Charles Edward's army and the lodging place of Captain Waverley 'in stirring '45'.

The only other place of public refreshment associated with Johnson in Edinburgh, or its neighbourhood, is the old inn at Roslin at which the bear's ward and the bear once stopped for a dish of tea on their way to Hawthornden. This stood on a site directly opposite the chapel, back from the road, and opinions are divided about whether it still exists or not. The original, described as being of grey stone, with a tiled roof, and little more than a cottage in size or condition, has certainly not survived unaltered.

The question naturally arises of how much Johnson's present fame stems from Boswell's ability as a biographer, as does its converse: 'How much of Boswell's fame depends on Johnson's greatness as a subject?' Everyone must admit that, despite his ineradicable prejudices, all Johnson's utterances both in writing and conversation, are stamped with the vigour, humour and good sense of his mind. Admittedly his *Dictionary* is no longer consulted, but when it first appeared in 1755 its

15

lucid definitions and extensive illustrations proved a new departure in lexicography. Again, his satirical verses, modelled upon those of Juvenal, are little read and his only novel, *Rasselas*, written to defray the expenses of his mother's funeral, is totally forgotten except by scholars. Yet his supremacy over the distinguished circle of his contemporaries is beyond question. Maybe it is true that if an obscure Scottish laird had not made a hero of him and worshipped him as no literary man has been worshipped before, or since, and if that laird had not written a biography which has been taken as a model for all others, he would have been forgotten completely and all his satellites with him. But since he has been preserved, a fly in amber, his essential humanity and sound judgement give permanent value to all his words. And we should not forget his own view of the enterprise which he expressed when he said to his earnest biographer, 'Sir, you have but two topics, yourself and me. I am sick of both.'

One of the most remarkable features of the biography, however, must be the exceedingly infrequent and limited personal meetings that there were between Boswell and Johnson—a fact frequently overlooked even by the most careful readers of the life. They first met about twenty years before Johnson's death; and after that meeting Boswell was not in England more than a dozen times. One expert has even counted the number of days when they were together in London, as well as during the visits to Edinburgh and the tour to the Hebrides, and has shown that they were together for only 276 days in all. So this marvellous biography, with its minuteness of detail, its small-talk and gossip, its wise and foolish disclosures, is the result of but nine months of actual observation of its subject by its author. A truly remarkable performance.

Boswell's house in James's Court, Lawnmarket, to which he conducted Johnson as soon as the new arrival had thrown the lemonade out of Lucky Boyd's window, and had threatened Boyd's waiter that he might follow it, is no longer in existence despite the claims of some guide books. James's Court, a little square, had three distinct entrances from the Lawnmarket, and was surrounded by houses eight or nine storeys in height. Robert Chambers thought that Boswell had two different suites of apartments in this court, and there is every reason to believe that as tenant of the earlier of these he succeeded the eminent historian and philosopher David Hume, who had gone there in 1762. This 'land' was, accidentally, totally destroyed by fire in 1857.

It was perhaps fortunate for Boswell's peace of mind that he had left Hume's old lodging before Johnson was his guest, for if Johnson had been told that the rooms he occupied had ever been profaned by the presence of 'that echo of Voltaire', it is to be feared that Mrs Boswell's tea, and Veronica herself, and all of the Boswell family, would have gone the way of Lucky Boyd's lemonade. When it was suggested that he should meet David Hume, Johnson's answer was a decided 'No, Sir!' He did expand on this a little later when he said of the famous philosopher, 'a man who has so much conceit as to tell all mankind that they have been bubbled for ages, and he is the wise man who sees better than they—a man who has so little scrupulosity as to venture to oppose those principles which have been thought necessary to human happiness—is he to be surprised if another man comes and laughs at him?' Boswell goes on to say, in the *Journal of a Tour to the Hebrides*, that Johnson 'added "*something much too rough*" both as to Mr Hume's head and heart. . . . Besides I always lived on good terms with Mr Hume, though I have frankly told him I was not clear that it was right in me to keep company with him. "But how much better are you than your books!" He was cheerful, obliging, and instructive; he was charitable to the poor; and

17

many an agreeable hour have I passed with him.' Boswell's attitude towards David Hume is very similar to that shown by the other men of the period who knew the philosopher. His own mother's opinion of him, however, was that 'Davy's a fine, good-natured crater, but uncommon wake-minded.'

Despite this maternal view, David Hume, historian, philosopher and sceptic was accepted by many as the greatest man of genius in Edinburgh at the time. This in no way diminishes his stature, for the city was described by Smollett in the late eighteenth century as 'a hotbed of genius'. Indeed, when Aymot, the king's dentist, was in Edinburgh he said as he stood at the Cross that at any minute he could take fifty men of genius by the hand.

Hume's first Edinburgh home was in Riddle's Close, on the opposite side of the Lawnmarket to James's Court. Writing of his removal here, Hume said: 'I have now at last—being turned of forty . . . arrived at the dignity of being a householder. About seven months ago I got a house of my own, and completed a regular family, consisting of a head, viz. myself, and two inferior members—a maid and a cat. My sister has since joined me, and keeps me company.' His house was 'in the first court reached on entering the close, and it is approached by a projecting turret stair'. It was here that Hume produced his *Political Discourses*, and little doubt can exist that he began to write his *History of England* here too, although the greater part of it was written in his house in Jack's Land, in the Canongate, to which he moved in 1753 and where he lived for nine years.

Jack's Land, now renumbered 229 Canongate, is an old four storeyed building entered from Little Jack's Close, and still stands much as Hume left it.

Although, in its day, Hume's *History of England* was ranked on a level with Gibbon's *Decline and Fall of the Roman Empire* it is now regarded more as a literary work than as a dependable

18

Hume's Lodgings, Riddle's Close, 322 High Street

treatise. But it is his work in philosophy—*A Treatise of Human Nature, Concerning Human Understanding,* and *The Principles of Morals*—developing the ideas of Locke and Berkeley, which has had the greatest effect and has greatly influenced European thought. His attitude to religion was one of profound scepticism and he thought that it arose 'from the incessant hopes and fears which actuate the human mind'. He was well known in Edinburgh as an atheist and was regarded by the inhabitants with solemn horror. On one occasion he was invited to dine at the house of Robert Adam, the famous architect. Adam's mother was very fond of speaking against the 'atheist' whom she had never seen. To play a trick upon her Adam placed her next to Hume without introducing him and afterwards she declared that 'the large, jolly man who sat next to me was the most agreeable of them all'. 'He was the very atheist, mother, that you were so afeared of,' said her son. 'Oh bring him here as much as you please, for he is the most innocent, agreeable, facetious man that I ever met with.' There can be no doubt that this description is just and it probably explains why there are so many legends and stories attached to his name. Most of these are quite obvious fabrications, like the tale that he was stuck in a bog under the Castle Rock and was only helped out by a passing Edinburgh dame on condition that he said the Lord's Prayer and the Creed, but a few have the ring of authenticity.

It is said that when he was young he paid court to a lady of fashion and was received with scant courtesy. A little later he was told that the lady had changed her mind. 'So have I,' said the philosopher. But he was not always so ungallant. When crossing the Firth of Forth, in a gale, with Lady Wallace, he observed that they would soon be food for fishes. 'Will they eat you or me?' she asked. 'Ah', was the answer, 'those that are gluttons will undoubtedly fall foul of me, but the epicures will attack your ladyship.' Hume, himself, was an epicure of the simplest kind and spent much of his time eating and drinking with the moderate clerics of the day in Johnny Dowie's tavern in Libberton's Wynd. Here he would sit of an evening with his huge door-key on the table before him, for his servant Peggy was always careful to see he had it so that she would not have to rise to let him in. Besides the drink, of which there was always more than sufficient, there would be a meal of haddock or tripe, fluke or pies, or maybe a fresh-caught trout—simple fare but excellently prepared, for Dowie's was famous for its little delicacies.

It is odd to think of Hume, the renowned atheist, sitting over his claret with the divines of the day, but they apparently thought his scepticism was mere pretence and subjected it to their ready wit. One day when he sat in the Poker Club it was mentioned that a clerk of Sir William Forbes, the banker, had run off with £900. It was reported that on his capture he was found to have Hume's *Treatise on Human Nature* in one pocket, and a work of evangelical theology in the other. All Hume's friends agreed that no man's morality could hold out against the combination. Not all the clerics of the period were so gentle in their criticism, however.

Hume originally despised the new town but eventually succumbed to its attraction and built himself a pretentious house at the corner of St Andrew Square, next to an unnamed street. According to one story, a mischievous young lady chalked up on the wall 'St David's Street'. When his maid-servant saw this inscription she rushed into her master's room in a fine state of indignation, only to be quietened with 'Never mind, lassie, mony a waur man has been made a saint o' before.' And St David's Street it remains.

His death was quiet, despite a well-meaning friend who asked him to 'burn a' yer wee bookies' and leave only the

History of England, and he was mourned by clerics and sceptics alike. A wild story of intrigue with the Devil spread rapidly around the town however, and his friends, fearing a violation of the grave, arranged to mount a vigil. This started at eight o'clock each evening with the firing of a pistol and the lighting of the candles in the lanterns, which were placed on the grave itself. They maintained their watch for eight nights but nothing untoward occurred. Today the simple round tower in the Calton burying ground, marking as it does a half-natural, half-artificial precipice, can be seen from many parts of the city —a reminder of one of the greatest thinkers Edinburgh has nurtured.

It is a curious coincidence that another historian of England should have lived for some time in a house directly opposite the house once occupied by Hume in the Canongate. Today, Tobias Smollett is not remembered for his history, but for his novels, especially *Roderick Random, Peregrine Pickle* and *Humphrey Clinker*, but he was a man of many parts.

Mrs Telfer, one of his sisters, occupied the second flat of 182 Canongate, over the archway leading into St John Street; and here the novelist spent some time in 1766. The house is little changed; the front windows look out upon the Canongate, although the apartments are now entered from that road through the first door to the right after passing the pend, and up the circular steps in the house now numbered 22 St John Street. It was here that, after a long absence, his mother recognized him by his smile. And it was also here that, when he came north again ten years later to see her, and tell her that he was very ill and probably dying, she said most Spartanly, 'We'll no' be very long pairted onie way. If you gang first, I'll be close on your heels. If I lead the way, you'll no be far ahint me.'

Robert Chambers, writing almost sixty years after this visit of Smollett to Edinburgh, described him as he had heard him

Smollett's House, St. John Street, Canongate

described by 'a person who recollects seeing him there'. He was 'dressed in black clothes, tall and extremely handsome, but quite unlike the portraits at the front of his works, all of which are disclaimed by his relations'.

St John Street also has artistic associations, for here Robert Strange, the engraver, lodged with other students in the Academy of Art run by Richard Cooper. As is usual with art students they were a noisy group and much given to pranks. The most notorious was Michael Hay who used to have Strange sleep with a string tied to his toe, with the other end dangling out of the window so that he could pull on it to have a rope lowered to him when he returned from his drinking excursions in the early hours of the morning. Strange eventually objected when, one night, he looked out of the window to see 'a young wench who was locked in the arms of my friend, and on my appearance he desired that I should give her admittance by throwing down the rope, swearing at the same time that he had brought her solely for my purpose'.

Strange was 'out' in the Forty-five—because of his love for Isabella Lumisden, sister to Prince Charles's secretary. Just before the disaster of Culloden, while he was staying in Inverness, Strange engraved the plates for the banknotes which the Jacobites wanted to issue, and delighted Prince Charles with his design incorporating the rose and the thistle and his suggestion that the date on which they fell due should be 'that of the Restoration'. He also engraved the only portrait of the Prince during the time he spent in Scotland. After Culloden, Strange was one of the many men hunted throughout the country and for some time he hid in Edinburgh. He was nearly caught, when visiting Isabella, by some soldiers who unexpectedly entered the house. Thinking quickly, his lady raised her hooped skirt and dropped it over her lover so that when the English came into the room all they found was a young lady singing quietly over her embroidery.

24

Smollett studied the Scottish capital and its inhabitants and introduced them both into *Humphrey Clinker,* first published in 1771. In this curious and ingenious commingling of facts and fancy, Smollett pictures himself as Matt Bramble and writes to 'Dr Lewis': 'Edinburgh is a hot-bed of genius; I have the good fortune to be made acquainted with many authors of the first distinction, such as the two Humes, Robertson, Smith, Wallace, Blair, Ferguson, Wilkie, etc., and I have found them all as agreeable in conversation as they are instructive and entertaining in their writings. These acquaintances I owe to the friendship of Dr Carlyle.'

All these are identifiable Edinburgh citizens of the time and they form part of the group that circled round Hume. Although none is as famous as the philosopher they are interesting since they enable us to visualize the way of life at the end of the eighteenth century.

Robertson was William Robertson, Doctor of Divinity, a historian, and rather a pompous man. He was the Principal of the University and a well known man of letters. He was frequently subject to mockery and one of his principal baiters was the son of the eminent Edinburgh doctor, William Cullen. Young Cullen was an excellent mimic and he not only imitated Robertson's voice and walk, but even his way of thought. It is said that Cullen once mimicked the doctor before some of the wits of the town about some matter that concerned him in the General Assembly. When he had finished the Principal walked in, and made the very same speech, only to be more than a little upset by the unaccountable hilarity it induced.

On another occasion a student who lodged with the Principal lay in bed recovering from some escapade when he heard a familiar footstep approach, and a familiar voice read him a lecture on his iniquities. He promised improvement in the future and lay back to rest again, when he heard the footsteps approach for the second time and the same lecture start all

25

over again. Up he jumped, and pulled aside the curtain shouting that it was too much to have the same thing twice over—only it was Robertson this time.

The Principal once went to Cullen's father for medical advice and was duly prescribed for. As he was leaving the doctor mentioned that he had just been giving the same advice, for the same complaint, to his own son.

Robertson died in 1793 in the Grange House, still standing south of the Grange Cemetery.

The Wallace mentioned by Smollett was Robert Wallace, another Doctor of Divinity, and famous in his own time as the author of *A Dissertation on the Numbers of Mankind*. Blair was Hugh Blair, yet another Doctor of Divinity, and very highly thought of by Doctor Johnson: 'I have read over Dr Blair's first sermon with more than approbation; to say it is good is to say too little.' He was noted for his vanity and the great care he took over his dress. As he walked to service in the High Kirk he was described as having 'his wig frizzed and powdered so nicely, his gown so scrupulously arranged on his shoulders, his hands so pure and clean, and everything about him in such exquisite taste and neatness'.

He once had his portrait painted and what with his efforts to smile pleasantly, to sweeten his forbidding countenance, and the painter's efforts to achieve a pleasing likeness, the resulting picture was hideous. Blair destroyed it in a fit of passion and commissioned a new one. For this less sublime results were aimed at, and the result did not rise above the commonplace.

Once an English visitor told him, before a small gathering, that his sermons were not popular among the southern clerics. Naturally all present expressed the greatest astonishment and Blair had the most piteous expression imaginable. This cleared remarkably quickly when the wit explained that this was

26

James's Court, 50 High Street

because 'they are so well known that none dare preach them'.

Blair was one of those responsible for introducing the poems of Ossian to a gullible world. He occupied Hume's apartments in James Court, when their owner was on the Continent, and he once lived in Argyle Square. He was buried in the Greyfriars Churchyard and his monument stands on the south side of the church.

Smollett's Wilkie was William Wilkie, another Doctor of Divinity. He was the author of a poem called the *Epigoniad* which achieved such fame that he was called 'the Scottish Homer' by Henry Mackenzie. So much for fame.

The Ferguson was Adam Ferguson, professor of moral philosophy at the university, and best remembered today for owning the house in which Burns met Scott for the first and only time.

Carlyle, in the eighteenth century, meant 'Jupiter' Carlyle—the Reverend Alexander Carlyle of Inveresk and Musselburgh who received the high accolade from one of his servants: 'There he gaed, dacent man, as steady as a wa' after his ain share o' five bottles of port.' Scott explained his nickname when he wrote 'The grandest demigod I ever saw, commonly called Jupiter Carlyle from having sat more than once for the King of Gods and men to Gavin Hamilton and a shrewd, clever old carle he was, no doubt, but no more a poet than his precentor.' This last remark refers to some doggerel rhyming which Carlyle once produced. He was one of the intimate cronies of David Hume and his *Autobiography* presents a graphic picture of the men of his time. In his later life he became unpopular in the church because of his assistance to Home in the production of *Douglas.*

The author of *The Wealth of Nations,* Adam Smith, is also included in Smollett's list. This is one of the most influential

28

books that has ever been written and its author was remarkable in many ways. Most of the stories about him dwell on his oblivion of everyday things—some think his indifference indicated contempt—and one of the best relates how the great economist scandalized a youthful visitor, and convulsed the drawing rooms of Edinburgh, by absently picking up a piece of bread and butter, rolling it round in his fingers, laying it in the teapot and pouring boiling water over it. Having tasted this extraordinary concoction, he announced solemnly that it was 'the worst tea he had ever met with'.

This incident occurred in his house in Panmure Close, in the Canongate, where he lived for the last twelve years of his life. After the last of his supper parties in this house, he rose, being very tired, but before retiring begged his guests to continue without him. At the door he turned and said gently, 'My friends, I fear I shall never see you again. But I trust we shall meet in another and a better world.' So he left them and his guests stayed on, discussing their host, his books, his wine, and his character. On the following Saturday he was dead. He was buried in the Canongate churchyard, a tall mural tablet on the wall of the rear of the courthouse, on the extreme left of the ground, recording the fact.

The house still stands, on the right-hand side of the close as one enters from the Canongate. It was restored and presented to the Canongate Boys' Club by Lord Thomson.

The 'two Humes' of whom Smollett wrote were unquestionably David Hume and John Home, the author of *Douglas,* as both of them were often in his society in Edinburgh. It is said that the closest approach to a disagreement in the long and intimate friendship existing between these 'two Humes' was regarding the relative merits of claret and port, and in relation to the spelling of their name, the philosopher in early life having adopted the orthography indicated by the pronunciation, the poet and preacher always clinging to the old and invariable custom of his family. David carried the discussion so far that on his death-bed he added a codicil to his will, written with his own hand, to this effect: 'I leave to my friend Mr John Home, of Kilduff, ten dozen of my old claret at his choice; and one other bottle of that other liquor called port. I also leave him six dozen of port, provided that he attests, under his hand, signed John *Hume,* that he has himself alone finished that bottle at a sitting. By this concession he will at once terminate the only difference that ever arose between us concerning temporal matters.'

John Home was born on the east side of Quality Street, near Bernard Street, Leith, in a house no longer standing. He was educated in the grammar-school of his native town, and at the University of Edinburgh. In 1767 he bought the farm of Kilduff, in East Lothian, where he remained until he removed to Edinburgh, thirteen years later. In Home's *Life and Letters* no hint is given as to his Edinburgh address. He died there, in 1808, and was buried in the yard of South Leith Parish Church, on the outer wall of which, on the south side, is a tablet with a simple inscription to his memory. It is visible, but not legible, from Kirkgate Street.

Douglas was first produced upon the regular stage on 14 December 1756, at the Canongate Theatre (of which there is no sign now), in Playhouse Close, 200 Canongate. According to tradition, however—and very misty tradition—it was performed privately some time before at the lodgings of Mrs Sarah Warde, a professional actress, who lived in Horse Wynd, near the foot of the Canongate, and with the following most astonishing amateur cast:

LORD RANDOLPH ...... Rev. Dr Robertson [principal of the University of Edinburgh].

GLENALVON ....Dr David Hume [historian].

OLD NORVAL............Rev. Dr Carlyle [minister of Mussel-
burgh].

DOUGLAS..................Rev. John Home [the author of the
tragedy].

LADY RANDOLPH......Dr Ferguson [professor of moral
philosophy in the University of Edin-
burgh].

ANNA (the Maid).......Rev. Dr Hugh Blair [minister of the
High Church of Edinburgh].

Adam Ferguson as Lady Randolph and Hugh Blair as Anna
must have added an unexpectedly comic element to the
tragedy. It is not more than justice to say that Dugald Stewart,
the biographer of Principal Robertson, asserts that the Randolph of this cast 'never entered a playhouse in his life'. On the
other hand, the Lady Randolph of this occasion, writing to
Home some years later, used very professional and rather
unfeminine language when she said: 'Dear John, damn the
actors that damned the play.' Lord and Lady Randolph, by the
way, were billed as Lord and Lady Barnet when *Douglas* was
originally produced, and the original Norval originally
declared his name to be 'Forman, on the Grampian Hills,' etc.

The first public performance of the play took place to a
packed house—the result of a mixture of scandal and curiosity
because it was the work of a Scottish divine, and the church had
been one of the main antagonists of the development of
theatre in Scotland. The tension on the first night was so great
that, on the sounding of the first bars of *Gill Morrice*—the song
upon which the play is based—all the ladies in the audience
burst into tears. *Douglas* became one of the most popular plays
of the century but the author was forced by the other divines to
relinquish his living and leave the church.

31

He still wanted to play a part in the General Assembly, how-ever, and he could not sit as a teaching elder—but he was Conservator of Scots privileges at Campvere which entitled him to sit as a ruling elder. He was also a lieutenant in the Duke of Buccleuch's Fencibles (the fencibles were a kind of militia raised for the defence of particular districts) and this meant that he had the right to wear a gorgeous uniform. Thus bedecked he took his seat in the reverend house, much to the amazement of the country ministers who stared with all their eyes. One of them exclaimed, 'Sure, that is John Home the poet! What is the meaning of that dress?' 'Oh,' said one of the Edinburgh men present, 'it is just the farce after the play.'

The play is now virtually forgotten, although it was revived with some success at the Edinburgh Festival recently but in the eighteenth century the comments on it were extreme. Even such a moderate man as David Hume said to the author, 'You possess the true theatrical genius of Shakespeare and Otway refined from the barbarisms of the one, and the licentiousness of the other.' In its day it was frequently performed and one of the most notable performances was given by Mrs Sarah Sid-dons during her visit to Edinburgh in 1784: 'there was not a dry eye in the whole house,' wrote the contemporary *Courant*. It must have been on this occasion that she dined with the Homes and asked in her best tragical manner for 'a little por-ter'. The old serving man left the room only to reappear carry-ing a diminutive caddie and saying 'I've found ane, mem; he's the least I could get!' Naturally everyone present laughed, but according to Robert Chambers the joke was lost on poor Mrs Home.

John's wife was a byword among his friends and they fre-quently pondered about why he had married someone who was neither clever, nor handsome, nor rich. David Hume asked him point-blank and received the very curious reply of 'Ah, David, if I had not who else would have taken her?'

Home's biographer was Henry Mackenzie, the 'Man of Feeling', whose opinions were accepted as the ultimate in sophistication by many in Edinburgh and who became its arbiter of taste. His best service to literature was his early public appreciation of Burns, but his novel *The Man of Feeling,* first published in 1771, was one of the greatest successes of the age and his other books, *The Man of the World* and *Julia de Roubigné* were highly praised. Admittedly Dr Johnson looked at a copy of *The Man of the World* when he was at Raasay and 'thought there was nothing in it' but Scott and Lockhart read him with admiration. Today his work seems extremely weak and overly sentimental, his style is stilted, and it is difficult to understand how he could have attained so great an influence in a society so studded with genius as Edinburgh at this time.

He earned his living as a lawyer but he was no dry-as-dust figure, for he was always keen to attend cock-fights. He once told his wife he had had a glorious night. 'Where?' she wondered. 'Why, at a splendid fight.' 'Oh, Harry, Harry,' came the retort, 'you only have feelings on paper.'

It is as a link between the different periods of Edinburgh's literary splendour that he attains his greatest importance. Born in 1745 in Libberton's Wynd, which ran north and south between the Lawnmarket and the Cowgate, where George IV Bridge now stands, he could remember the figures of Allan Ramsay and Robert Fergusson and he was, himself, in his old age, a familiar figure in nineteenth-century Edinburgh. Like so many of his townsfolk he was educated in the High School and the University. He had many residences in Edinburgh during his long life of which some still survive. The tenement now known as 36 Chambers Street was his home for many years, although it was then called 4 Brown Square. The last years of his life were passed at 6 Heriot Row, in one of a long

33

line of eminently 'genteel' houses facing the Queen Street Gardens, ground over which he had shot as a boy.

Mackenzie's writings contain a few episodes which cast an interesting light on the haphazardness of life in the city of his day. The houses were frequently built between two wynds and had an entry in each. When Edinburgh was a wilder place this was probably a useful precaution, but by the eighteenth century it had outlived its usefulness. Mackenzie wrote in some autobiographical notes, 'I remember a mistake of a lady's chairmen carrying her, first to a wrong door in one wynd, when she was ushered into a drawing-room where, when she discovered her mistake, she made her apology and returned to her chair, the bearers of which were directed to the house she wished to go to, of which the proper door was in the other wynd. She was carried thither accordingly but unluckily to the other entry of the very house she had left, and on being admitted was ushered into the self-same drawing-room.'

The people were, in many ways, as haphazard in their attitudes, frequently being both devout and profane, like the gentleman with whom Mackenzie once dined. He rose to say grace, realized too late that he should have allowed a clergyman who was present have the honour and said 'Oh Lord! . . . God's curse! . . . Deil care! . . . Amen!'

Another of his stories shows how firm a place was occupied by Mary Stuart in the Edinburgh of his time. David Hume wanted a book from the Advocates' Library, which was in a court off the Lawnmarket. The acting librarian was a man called Goodall, who was the author of the first tract which attempted to act as a vindication of Mary. When Hume arrived at the library Goodall 'was sitting in his elbow-chair so fast asleep that neither David nor a friend who accompanied him could wake Goodall by any of the normal means'. At last David said, 'I think I have a method of waking him,' and bawled into

34

his ear, 'Queen Mary was a strumpet and a murtherer—' 'It's a damned lie,' said Goodall, starting out of his sleep . . .' and Hume got his book.

Mackenzie died in Heriot Row in 1831 and now lies under a plain mural tablet in the Greyfriars Churchyard, on the north side of the terrace. It describes him 'as an author who for no short time and in no small part supported the literary reputation of his country'—it is slightly ironic that the only shrine in Greyfriars' which visitors now care for is the grave of a man of whom nothing is known except that his single mourner was a mongrel.

A neighbour of Mackenzie's in Greyfriars, and now almost equally forgotten by the world, is Allan Ramsay, and yet it was said that when he died Scottish poetry died with him. Unlike Mackenzie, however, this neglect is unjust for Ramsay was the moving spirit in the revival of Scottish poetry, and it was in many ways because of his efforts in the early eighteenth century that social life, poetry, conviviality and conversation found their happy union in the small intimate groups of the literary clubs.

He began his life in Edinburgh as an apprentice to a wig-maker in 1701 but by 1718 he had become a bookseller who tried to meet the intellectual requirements of the capital. By 1720 he was also a publisher and his books bear an imprint indicating that they were sold 'at the sign of the Mercury, opposite the head of Niddry's Wynd'.

In 1726 he moved from this shop to one on the second floor of a building which stood upon the line of the High Street, 'alongside St Giles's Church', his windows commanding the City Cross and the lower part of the High Street. Here he changed his sign, substituting the heads of Ben Jonson and Drummond of Hawthornden for that of Mercury; and here, in 1728, he added to his business a circulating library, the first in Scotland.

This was viewed very seriously by all pious persons and the Reverend Robert Wodrow stigmatized it in the following familiar terms: 'All the villainous, profane, and obscene books and plays, as printed in London, are got down by Allan Ramsay and lent out, for an easy price, to young boys, servant weemen of the better sort, and gentlemen . . . by these wickedness of all kinds are dreadfully propagat among the youths of all sort. . . . A villainous obscene thing is no sooner printed at London than it is spread and communicat at Edinburgh.'

Not that all this might not be true, for Allan Ramsay was not only the poet of *The Gentle Shepherd* and the *Tea-Table Miscellany* but a famous celebrator of the pleasures of the bottle, and sometimes of the flesh. There are those that consider his verse too strong for polite society even today.

> Then fling on coals and ripe the ribs,
> And beek the house baith but and ben,
> That mutchkin stoup it hauds out dribs,
> Then let's get in the tappit hen.
>
> Good claret best keeps out the cauld,
> And drives away the winter sune;
> It makes a man baith gash and bauld,
> And heaves his saul beyond the mune.

Allan Ramsay was at his best in this type of drinking song and it is difficult to beat this example for vigour. But it is more than likely that he sang about drinking more than doing it and his cronies must have shouted 'Pike yer bane' without success at the little 'black-a-vised' man wearing a nightcap for a hat. Some of his best work is in the form of mock elegies for innkeepers like Maggie Johnson, who kept a famous 'howf' of Bruntsfield links:

36

> There we got fou wi' little cost
>> And muckle speed.
> Now wae worth Death! our sport's a' lost
>> Since Maggy's dead!

or Luckie Wood, who kept an equally celebrated house in the Canongate,

> She ne'er gae in a lawin fause,
>> Nor stoups a' froath aboon the hause,
> Nor kept dow'd tip within her waws,
>> But reaming swats.
> She ne'er ran sour jute, because
>> It gees the batts.

Later in the century the shop on the ground floor, under Ramsay's, belonged to William Creech, who published the second, or 'Edinburgh', edition of Burns' poems in 1787, and the tenement was therefore called Creech's Land—a fact that has given some former writers severe problems. It was part of the Luckenbooths, which have long since been removed. These 'locked booths' were squeezed into the space between the Church and the High Street's northern side and have been described as 'a group of queer-looking buildings which stood in, not on, the High Street, blocking up and disfiguring that thoroughfare'.

The Gentle Shepherd was written and published while Ramsay was trading, and living too, in his establishment opposite Niddry's Wynd—now Niddry Street—and the house stood until one of the reconstructions of the North Bridge encroached upon it and swept it away. It was one of the most interesting of the old buildings in Edinburgh at the end of the nineteenth century. It only had two storeys, since the gables that had formerly surmounted it had been removed, but it was topped by a high and steeply sloping roof from which rose an enormous square chimney, that might have passed, as one writer said, 'for a cupola or bell tower in the frequent mists of the place'. All that now remains are a few relics, mostly ornamental reliefs, which are displayed on the National Commercial Bank.

The last years of Ramsay's life were passed in the house he built on the Castle Hill. Apparently Ramsay applied to the Crown for as much ground from the Hill as would serve him to build a cage for his *burd*, meaning his wife, to whom he was warmly attached, and the resulting grant is supposed to account for the octagonal shape, because the poet was not willing to let any of the ground go to waste. He was extremely proud of his new mansion and was somewhat surprised that its fantastic shape excited the mirth, rather than the admiration, of his fellow citizens. The wags of the town compared it to a goose-pie and when he complained of this to Lord Elibank, his lordship replied, 'Indeed, Allan, when I see you in it I think they are not far wrong.' The house still survives, somewhat overgrown by later building, as part of the picturesque group of houses beneath the Castle Esplanade which still retain some of the distinctive features of 'denty Allan's' cosy little villa.

In 1736 Ramsay opened his ill-fated theatre in Carruber's Close, now completely obliterated but in those days close to the 'sign of the Mercury'. It did not long survive the strictures of the Kirk and soon became St Andrew's Chapel. Today the site is occupied by a distillery—the Kirk's attitude towards the relative merits of whisky and plays is not recorded.

Allan Ramsay, the poet's son, made great changes to the 'Goose Pie' when it came into his possession after his father's death in 1758. The young Allan Ramsay was then at the height of his powers and many of his greatest portraits—*Mrs Bruce of Arnot, the Duke of Atholl,* and *Hew Dalrymple,* for example—date from this period. Born in 1713, he showed his artistic talent while still very young, and his father encouraged him and saw

38

that he was given assistance and patronage. In 1736 his father wrote to an artist friend, 'My son Allan has been pursuing your science since he was a dozen years old; was with Mr Halliday at London for some time about two years ago; has been since at home, painting here like a Raphael; out for the seat of the Beast beyond the Alps within a month hence, to be away two years.' This journey to Rome was, presumably, financed by his father's friends and patrons and soon after his return he established his position firmly—despite the jealousy and opposition of the many fashionable portrait painters in London. Among his clients was Lord Bute and so successful was his full-length portrait that even Reynolds took particular pains over a portrait he was doing at the time, saying 'I wish to show legs with Ramsay's Lord Bute.'

Ramsay quickly became a favourite among the rich and famous—even Johnson had a good word to say for him—and he was undoubtedly a most charming person, being a scholar, a wit and a gentleman. One result of this charm was the commission to paint George III and his Queen in their coronation robes in 1760, which was followed in 1767 by his appointment to be Painter-in-Ordinary to the King. Since he could speak German, a rare accomplishment in the court circles of the time, he was able to talk with both the king and queen in a language of which they had a rather better command than English—which must have furthered his position as well. But Ramsay also fell in with the king's homely ways and it is reputed that when the king had finished eating his favourite dinner of boiled mutton and turnips he would say, 'Now Ramsay, sit down in my place and take your dinner.'

George III was particularly fond of presenting copies of the coronation portrait to visitors and Ramsay had to provide a ready supply. This meant production in his Harley Street studios almost on a factory scale and while, initially, Ramsay had painted the heads and hands himself, and even put in a few final touches on some, as the numbers grew his interest declined until at last the final copies have little from his hand. By 1775 his pupil Reinagle had become so expert that Ramsay had little to do except superintend. So Ramsay went off to Italy 'for his health' leaving instructions for his assistant to get ready fifty pairs of kings and queens at ten guineas a time. As Reinagle painted the commonplace faces of George and his wife Charlotte Sophia over and over again, he gradually became so sick of the whole business that he struck for more pay. Ultimately he trebled his fee but in later life he always looked back on the period as a horrid nightmare.

One day Allan Ramsay the painter visited the coach builder Crighton and was so struck by the coat of arms painted by one of the apprentices that he persuaded the boy's employer to waive his rights and release the boy from his indentures. Alexander Nasmyth thus became one of Ramsay's pupils and stayed with him until 1778.

Nasmyth was born in a house in the Grassmarket in 1758. This was, at that time, the busy centre of Edinburgh traffic and it was frequently full of sheep and cattle for the fairs. Directly opposite his birthplace stood the inn from which the coach left for Newcastle 'ilka Tuesday at Twa o'clock in the day, GOD WULLIN', but *whether or no* on Wednesday'. As a boy one of his favourite tricks was to take a barrel to the top of the Castle Hill, fill it with small stones, and then shoot it down towards the roofs of the houses in the Grassmarket. The barrel would leap from rock to rock until, at last, it would burst and shower the stones far and wide. But the best part to the fun was to see the 'boddies' look out of their garret windows with lamps and candles and peer into the dark to try to see the cause of the mischief.

In 1778 Nasmyth returned to Edinburgh where he set up as

40

a portrait-painter, and soon obtained ample employment including a portrait for Patrick Miller of Dalswinton. Miller was a retired banker and spent his time in experiments in agriculture and steam propulsion. Nasmyth was gifted with a very ingenious mind and soon the pair of them were deep in designing mechanically powered boats. The fruit of their labours was a successful voyage on Dalswinton Loch, in a boat constructed from tinned iron plate and propelled by a paddle driven by steam, on 14 October 1788, when they carried as one of their passengers the poet Robert Burns.

Nasmyth lived in St James's Square during the early years of his marriage but moved to 47 York Place, a house he designed for himself, at about the time that he changed to landscape painting. This was forced upon him to a certain extent because of his political opinions, which led to a decline in the number of sitters, but he succeeded so well in his new endeavour that he is often referred to as the 'father of Scottish landscape'.

An all-round man, he indulged in mechanics and architecture (being particularly interested in the design of the New Town), painted stage scenery and carried out many commissions as a landscape gardener. One of his more endearing exploits in the last art was to plant trees and shrubs on some inaccessible crags by firing seeds from a small cannon. His large family were all talented artists, Patrick the eldest son in particular, while James Nasmyth is best known for the invention of the steam-hammer.

Nasmyth's pupils included John Thomson of Duddingston, where he was parish minister from 1805 to 1840. He is alleged to have received his first lessons in art from the carpenter of the village where he was born. He was very friendly with Scott, who was a frequent visitor, and Turner came to see him—only to make the typical remark, 'Ah, Thomson, you beat me hollow—in frames.' His studio, built at the end of the manse garden, was called Edinburgh so that his housekeeper could ward off unwelcome callers truthfully by saying he had gone there.

Another, much later, artist who had fond memories of Duddingston and its loch was Sir William Russell Flint. He was born in 1880 at Lutton Place and spent his boyhood in the city, being apprenticed at the age of fourteen to Banks and Co., the printers. When winter frosts froze the lochs it was the custom for the firms' artist apprentices to be given a skating half holiday which was much appreciated. He wrote in his autobiography, *In Pursuit*, 'One winter there was a splendid six-week spell of skating. Duddingston Loch was our favourite resort and memorable were the moonlight nights when the ice skirled and rang under the steel-shod swirling hordes . . . It was high carnival under the sombre crags of Arthur's Seat.' How many of today's apprentices will be able to have similar memories?

From 1810 the house at 47 York Place had, as one of its tenants, Andrew Geddes, who was just starting his practice as a portrait-painter. He was born in Edinburgh in 1783 but his father had attempted to prevent the son following an artistic career and made him enter the Excise Office. His father's death came in 1803 and Andrew Geddes went to London in 1806, where he became friendly with another expatriate Scot— David Wilkie.

At the age of fourteen Wilkie came up to Edinburgh to try for entry to the Trustees Academy. The secretary, George Thomason, examined his drawings and declared that they were not of sufficient merit to warrant his admission, but the Earl of Leven insisted that he must be admitted and so he was. His early efforts in the drawing-class seem to have been undistinguished. Indeed when his father showed one of his studies to a neighbour, he faced the question, 'What is it?' But his

42

reply, 'A foot,' was met with 'A fute! A fute! it's mair like a fluke a fute!'

After five years in Edinburgh, Wilkie returned to his home in Cults, Fife, where he started painting *Pitlessie Fair.* One Sunday he saw an ideal character nodding to sleep in one of the pews during his father's sermon and he quickly made a sketch on the flyleaf of his Bible. Other eyes were watching, however, and he was taken to task. He managed to mollify his accusers with the sheer cheek of his excuse—that in sketching only the hand and eye were engaged and that he could hear and absorb the sermon at the same time. Even his father did not escape Wilkie's brush and is shown talking amicably to the publican— about which he complained bitterly to the young artist.

One of the poet Ramsay's frequent haunts was Jenny Ha's Change House and here, in 1729, there could often be seen 'a pleasant young man in a tie wig'—John Gay, the author of

How happy I could be with either
Were t'other dear charmer away

who had walked up the Canongate to enjoy a conversation with the author of

Wae's me! For baith I canna get
To ane by law we're stented;
Then I'll draw cuts, and take my fate,
And be with ane contented.

And sitting in the window of the Change House with a warming drink, Allan Ramsay would point out to Gay the leading citizens as they passed in the street below. This was John Gay's only visit to Edinburgh and he was brought as the secretary (and special protégé) of the duchess of Queensberry. The Lord Chamberlain had refused a licence to *Polly,* Gay's sequel to *The Beggar's Opera,* because some of the members of the government had been satirized in it. So 'her mad Grace of

Queensberry' had packed Gay, and her husband, into a coach and six and hustled them all up to Edinburgh and to Queensberry House—a tall four-storeyed building set in extensive lawns, which is now used for housing the elderly and chronically sick. Tradition has it that Gay did not stay in this great pile but lodged in the upper storey of a poor tenement opposite it, not far from Jenny Ha's establishment.

But the duchess did not let them stay long together, for she quickly swallowed her pride and swept her husband and her protégé back to London to stir up more scandal with her mad pranks.

Another temporary resident of this time was Oliver Goldsmith, who was a medical student at the university in 1752. It is said that he lived in College Wynd, the remains of which survive as the zigzag Guthrie Street. He wrote several accounts of the General Assemblies that were held during this period and their dullness and formality turns, in his hands, to an amusing drollery. Goldsmith can be imagined parading the streets of the Old Town dressed in the suit of sky-blue satin and black velvet, topped with a 'superfine small hatt' that carried '8s worth of silver hatt lace' which appears on a tailor's bill found during the last century. He also purchased, from the same tailor, a 'superfine high claret coloured' cloth suit but it is unknown whether poor Mr Filby, the tailor, ever saw his money or not, because the bill was carried over.

From 1785 on, the professor of moral philosophy in the University of Edinburgh was Dugald Stewart, the son of a previous professor of mathematics. He was a disciple of Hume's opponent, Thomas Reid—the author of an *Enquiry into the Human Mind on the Principle of Common Sense*. Stewart was not a brilliant philosopher but he managed to transmit the idea of a liberal culture to his students, basing it on self-knowledge, taste, and 'moral sensibility'—a typical eighteenth-century formulation of the parts that made a gentleman. One of his students wrote, 'To me his lectures were like the opening of the heavens. I felt I had a soul. His noble views, unfolded in glorious sentences, elevated me into a higher world. I was as much excited and charmed as any man of cultivated taste would be who, after, being ignorant of their existence, was admitted to all the glories of Milton, and Cicero, and Shakespeare. They changed my whole nature.'

His superior command of linguistic style combined with his own shining example to excite an interest in philosophy such as had never been known previously in England and Scotland. The same student also wrote, 'No intelligent pupil of his ever ceased to respect philosophy or was ever false to his principles, without feeling the crime aggravated by the recollection of the morality that Stewart had taught him.'

Not that Stewart was without his faults, one of which, it is alleged, was to forget to return books which he had borrowed, perhaps from the absence of mind typical of a philosopher. One of the Edinburgh wits, when he heard the professor confess that, eminent as he was in many branches of knowledge, he was deficient in Arithmetic, riposted 'That, tho' very improbable might be true; but he certainly excels in Book-Keeping.'

Stewart lived for many years in 'Lothian Hut', erected in 1750 by William, third Marquis of Lothian, in the Horse Wynd, Canongate (reputedly so called because it was the only throughfare leading from the southern suburbs which a horse could descend safely) and he wrote several of his most notable works there. But the site is now occupied by a brewery. He later moved to Whitefoord House, which still survives in its position almost opposite Queensberry House, before he moved to 7 Moray Place where he died. It was in this last residence that the second Mrs Stewart dispensed the hospitality for which she became celebrated. She had met the philosopher after her cousin, the Earl of Lothian, had shown him a poem written by her. Stewart was the earl's tutor and expressed his criticism in most flattering terms. The result was that the philosopher fell in love with the poetess, and she loved him for his eulogy. Their marriage could not have been more successful.

She must have been a most remarkable woman and one of her friends has left a description of her. 'Though the least beautiful of a family in which beauty is hereditary, she had the best essence of beauty, expression, a bright eye beaming with intelligence, a manner the most distinguished yet soft, feminine and winning. She bestowed a wealth of affection on her husband which was beautiful to witness. Her grace and dignity made a great impression on the pupils who were placed under the professor's care, many of whom attained the highest honours in political life—Lords Palmerston, Lansdowne, Dudley, Kinnaird, and Ashburton. Her talent, wit and beauty made the wife of the professor one of the most attractive women in the city. No wonder, therefore, that her *salons* were the resort of all that was best of Edinburgh.'

It was Dugald Stewart who, returning from a holiday spent in Ayrshire where he had met the poet, carried back with him a copy of the Kilmarnock edition of the poems of Robert Burns which he lent to Henry Mackenzie. The outcome was the famous review in the *Lounger*. Stewart was one of the people whom Burns came to know best in Edinburgh and his description of the philosopher is not without interest.

'An exalted judge of the human heart, and of composition. One of the very first public speakers; and equally capable of generosity as humanity. His principal discriminating feature is: from a mixture of benevolence, strength of mind, and manly dignity, he not only at heart values, but in his deportment and address bears himself to all the Actors, high and low,

46

in the drama of Life, simply as they might merit in playing their parts. Wealth, honours, and all that is extraneous of the man, have no more influence with him than they will have at the Last Day.'

This paragon of the eighteenth-century virtues lies close to Adam Smith in the Canongate Churchyard, near the south-west corner under a large altar tomb of grey stone. Two other notable Scots are also buried there—'the two Fergusons', Robert and Adam, who were much further apart in life than they are in death.

Even those who have heard of Robert Fergusson frequently consider him as merely a forerunner of Burns but, considering that he was just twenty-four when he died, lonely and miserable, in the pauper lunatic asylum called Old Darien House, he has many claims to be regarded as one of Britain's most remarkable poets.

Robert Fergusson was born in 1750 in Cap and Feathers Close, the site of which is now covered by the buildings standing on the east side of the North Bridge. He went to a small school in Niddry's Wynd (now Niddry Street) and later went to the first High School. As a young man he was severely censured by contemporary society for his dissolute behaviour and this may, in part, account for his unjust neglect. Mackenzie's attitude is clear when he describes him as being 'dissipated and drunken' and mentions his having produced 'poems faithfully and humorously describing scenes of Edinburgh of festivity and somewhat of blackguardism'. Of course, this may be only pique because of Fergusson's satire on him as *The Sow of Feeling*.

Fergusson was probably no worse than his companions and it may be that they could stand more than he could. For in his world a 'fine fellow' was a man who could drink three bottles at a sitting, as Creech the bookseller observed, and who ridiculed religion and morality as folly and hypocrisy. It was made up of men who had failed in the various professions, or who had taken to drink instead of to work. They lived on the edge of the Edinburgh underworld, in a vicious Grub Street, all more or less clever, all poor, all drunken, and all ready to do anything for a dram. There is no record of the conversation that must have flowed and sparkled over the glasses—society recorded the wit of a judge after his three bottles of claret, but not that of the wastrels, no matter how brilliant.

The poet once gave as an excuse for his behaviour 'oh sirs, anything to forget my poor mother and these aching fingers,' which is a poor enough excuse for forgetting himself. But we should not be too hard on the youth who had to leave St Andrew's University, after the death of his father, to support his mother and who had to drudge his days away in the uncongenial atmosphere of a law office.

> But law is a draw-well unco deep,
>   Withouten rim fock out to keep;
> A donnart chiel, whan drunk, may dreep
>   Fu' sleely in,
> But finds the gate baith stay and steep
>   Ere out he win.*

It is as a poet of the town, a recorder of urban sights and manners, that Fergusson excels. This is not to say that his poems about the countryside are inaccurate in the observation of detail, but, excellent as poems like 'The Farmer's Ingle' are, they do not have the deep personal feeling of the town poems. The pictures he sketches of life in Edinburgh are particularly vivid:

* unco = remarkably; fock = folk; donnart chiel = foolish fellow; dreep = drop; sleely = easily; gate = way; stay = hard to climb.

Now morn, with bonny purpie-smiles,
   Kisses the air-cock o' St Giles;
Rakin' their ein, the servant lasses
   Early begin their lies and clashes;
Ilk tells her friend of saddest distress,
   That still she brooks frae scolding mistress;
And wi' her joe in turnpike stair
   She'd rather snuff the stinking air,
As be subjected to her tongue,
   When justly censur'd in the wrong.*

He sees the seamy side of Edinburgh, as well, but he does not moralize, rather he presents the complex diversity of the city's day as it is, embracing all the senses.

Near some lamp-post, wi' dowy face,
   Wi' heavy ein, and sour grimace,
Stands she that beauty lang had kend,
   Whoredom her trade, and vice her end . . .
And sings sad music to the lugs,
   'Many burachs o' damn'd whores and rogues . . .†

The ordinary people have his greatest sympathy, as one would expect, and when he writes of them he is at his gentlest.

In afternoon, a' brawly buskit,
   The joes and lasses loe to frisk it:
Some tak a great delight to place
   The modest *bon-grace* o'er the face;
Tho' you may see, if so inclin'd,
   The turning o' the leg behind.
Now Comely-Garden, and the Park,
   Refresh them, after forenoon's wark . . .‡

* purpie = purple; ein = eyes; clashes = gossip; ilk = each; joe = sweetheart; as = than.
† dowy = fatigued; lang had kend = had known long ago; lugs = ears; burach = crowd.
‡ brawly buskit = dressed in their best clothes; loe = love; *bon-grace* = bonnet.

But it is perhaps as a poet of Edinburgh in winter that he is at his most vivid:

Cauld blaws the nippin north wi' angry sough,
  And showers his hailstanes frae the Castle Cleugh
O'er the Greyfriars . . .*

Fergusson must have really suffered from these cold blasts and this may be considered as some excuse for his love of the taverns with their cosiness, entertaining company and friendly talk.

When big as burns the gutters rin,
  Gin ye hae catcht a droukit skin,
To Lucky Middlemist's lowp in,
  And sit fu' snug
O'er oysters and a dram o' gin,
  Or haddock lug.†

Lucky Middlemist's tavern was long ago replaced by the south pier of the South Bridge and a similar fate has followed all the taverns and clubs which were the poet's favourite resorts. He lived in an Edinburgh where nothing could be done without a dram and even the bells of St Giles, as they tolled the hours, were called the 'gill' bells. The 'meridian' followed the 'morning' and both only prepared the honest men of the town for the serious drinking of the evening. Admittedly most of the drink consumed was only claret but huge jugs of the wine were carried in every direction up and down the streets of Edinburgh, much as ale jugs were in London. Whenever a ship arrived from Bordeaux the hogsheads of claret were carried through the town and set up in the streets so that the people could fill their jugs straight from the spigot at a very cheap rate.

When we consider the conditions under which even quite

* cleugh = cliff.
† Gin = if; droukit = wet; lowp = jump.

respectable people were forced to live, it is not surprising that taverns were in such great use. To live outside the town was not considered fashionable and this led to the construction of the towering 'lands', or tenements, of fourteen and even fifteen storeys, with all their attendant inconveniences. All the water that a family needed, for example, had to be carried up the narrow twisting stairs and cleanliness cost too much of an effort for many. The height also meant that all household refuse and slops had either to be carried down the stairs or thrown from the windows. This was a constant peril after dark since one never knew when, following (and sometimes preceding) the warning cry of 'Gardyloo'—a corruption of the French *Gardez à l'eau*—a torrent of filth would pour on to the footpath, or the pedestrian. In *Humphrey Clinker* Smollett makes Winifred Jenkins write, 'All the "chairs" in the family are emptied into this here barrel once a day; and at ten o'clock at night the whole charge is flung out of a back window that looks into some street or lane, and the maid cries "Gardyloo" to the passengers, which means, *Lord have mercy upon you!* This is done every night in Haddinborough, so you may guess, Mary Jones, what a sweet savour comes from such a number of perfumery pans. But they say it is wholesome.'

Some of the tallest houses in old Edinburgh were like vertical streets and contained nearly as many families, crammed into the space from cellar to roof, as a normal street in any other town. The richer and better born citizens lived on the second or third floors of the lands to avoid the odours of the street, while the lower floors were occupied by scavengers and poorly-paid clerks, and the floors above them would be lived in by shopkeepers and the merchants. The very highest points in these buildings, the garrets and attics, were the homes of the artisans and labourers. All these people were forced into the closest contact and they could not avoid meeting on the twisty stairs, which led to the development of an atmosphere of communal friendliness.

Even though they could afford the best situations in the tenements, the aristocrats, professional men and people of independent means, frequently had to be content with a mere two or three rooms in which all their public and private life had to be performed. A leading lawyer of the time, Bruce of Kennet, lived in a flat of three rooms—a parlour, consulting room, and bedroom—and a kitchen. The children had their beds made for them every night in the consulting room, where they slept with their maid. The housemaid slept under the kitchen dresser and the one man servant had to find lodgings of his own because there was no room for him.

This shortage of accommodation meant that everyone had to use the taverns to a far greater extent than now. A barrister would meet his clients in one, and a doctor his patients. Almost every tradesman had a favourite corner in a choice tavern where, once he had completed his day's business, he would sit with the door of his booth closed, for the taverns were divided into peculiar little separate boxes which threw an air of secrecy and mystery over all the meetings that took place within them. Inside this 'private room' he would eat his supper, of haddock, collops or sheep's head, and crack a joke with his friends over a bottle or two before going home for the night.

One of the most famous taverns was Johnny Dowie's in Libberton's Wynd, which was a favourite resort of Robert Fergusson, and later Robert Burns, as well as so many other famous names that it has been called 'The Mermaid of Edinburgh'. But when the George IV Bridge was built both tavern and wynd were swept away and, like everything else associated with Fergusson in life, there is no trace of it left. We do not even possess an absolutely authetic portrait of him and the best, if the most homely, of contemporary descriptions represents him as being 'very smally and delicate, a little in-kneed, and waigled a good deal in walking'. Presumably the 'waigling' came from a session at one of the clubs, like the Cape Club, where on so many occasions 'wi' sang and glass he'd flee the power o' care, that wad harass the hour'. The Cape Club was undoubtedly his favourite and it met at the Isle of Man's Arms in Craig's Close.

This was just one of the many clubs—political, literary, sporting, scientific, and just plain drinking—that proliferated throughout Edinburgh. Their origins can be traced back to Allan Ramsay's circle of literati who met in his circulating library to discuss the ways of the world but, by the end of the eighteenth century, no joke was too trivial, no custom too ridiculous, to be seized upon as a pretext for founding a club. The Cape Club (all of whose members took fanciful titles and viewed each other as noble knights) was, reputedly, so-called because of the difficulties some members had in turning the sharp corner ('doubling the cape') at the end of the wynd in which it was situated. This must rank as a relatively sensible reason for naming a club in a city which had a Pious Club (because its members met to eat pies) and a Spendthrift Club (whose members were not allowed to spend more than fourpence-halfpenny). Doubtless the Salt Herring Club and the Odd Club were innocent but the meetings of the Sweating Club, the Dirty Club and the Ten Tumbler Club must only have been excuses for licence and riot. The Catch Club had what Henry Mackenzie calls the 'beastly custom' of Saving the Ladies which involved drinking more than a quart of punch at one draught. This, not surprisingly, frequently acted as an emetic and this result was probably regarded as the biggest joke possible by the hard drinkers who gathered together in such surroundings.

Bottle wit is, however, like the fizz from champagne, and despite all the famous men that were members of these clubs,

53

and all the gallant talk that must have echoed through the taverns, little now remains but a memory preserved in the poems of Fergusson and Burns. How far Burns was really influenced by the poetry of Fergusson is difficult to say but he certainly regarded him very highly. When one of his neighbours, William Simpson of Ochiltree, praised his talents as a poet, Burns replied:

> My senses wad be in a creel,
> Should I but dare a hope to speel,
> Wi' Allan, or wi' Gilbertfiel',
> The braes o' fame;
> Or Fergusson, the writer-chiel,
> A deathless name.

By placing himself below Allan Ramsay and William Hamilton of Gilbertfield, Burns was certainly underestimating his own ability, but he recognized, more than many Scots have done, Fergusson's very real ability. Typically Burns goes on to hit at the Edinburgh gentry who allowed a native genius to die insane and in poverty.

> O Fergusson! thy glorious parts
> Ill suited law's dry, musty arts!
> My curse upon your whunstane hearts,
> Ye Enbrugh Gentry!
> The tythe o' what ye waste at cartes
> Wad stow'd his pantry!

Certainly one of the first places he went to when he visited Edinburgh in the winter of 1786–7 was to the Canongate cemetery where he searched for Fergusson's grave. And when he found it, he wrote to the Honourable Bailies of Canongate: 'I am sorry to be told that the remains of Robert Fergusson, the so justly celebrated poet, a man whose talents for ages to come

54

will do honour to our Caledonian name, lie in your churchyard among the ignoble dead, unnoticed and unknown. Some memorial to direct the steps of the lovers of Scottish song when they wish to shed a tear over the narrow house of the bard who is now no more is surely a Tribute due to Fergusson's memory—a Tribute I wish to have the honour of paying. I petition you, then, gentlemen, to permit me to lay a simple stone over his reverend ashes, to remain an unalienable property to his deathless fame.'

The stone with its unpretentious inscription

Here lies Robert Fergusson, Poet, born 5th Sept 1751
died 16th October 1774

No sculptur'd marble here, nor pompous lay.
  'No storied urn, nor animated bust';
This simple stone directs pale Scotia's way
  To pour her sorrow o'er her Poet's dust.

is on the west side of the church, not many steps from the gateway and on the left as one enters the churchyard. It is always well cared for, and a royal Scottish thistle, planted by some devout hand, rises, as if defiantly, to guard the spot, which has been honoured by the raising of many hats in reverence, for Burns' sake if not for Fergusson's.

Robert Burns had come to Edinburgh following the success of the Kilmarnock Edition of his poems. The first edition had appeared early in August and had been so eagerly sought for by his local friends and even 'the first Gentlemen of the County' that by the end of the month only thirteen copies remained unsold out of the edition of 612. This occurred while he was being pursued by Old Armour as a result of his affair with Jean Armour and one of Burns's plans to avoid the inconveniences of his indiscretions was to flee to Jamaica. He had

55

been advised to sail in a Captain Cathcart's ship, the *Bell*, due to leave Greenock for Kingston at the end of September. Apparently he set off for Greenock but on the way he called on the Reverend George Lawine, the minister of Loudon, Newmilns, who welcomed him warmly and perhaps told the poet of his intention to write to Dr Thomas Blacklock, the blind but influential poet, about the Kilmarnock poems. His interest in the reaction of one of the leading literati of Edinburgh may have swayed Burns and made him decide against joining the *Bell* but he let her sail away without him.

The reply, when it came, expressed great enthusiasm for the poems, or rather it expressed as much enthusiasm as the formality of its style allowed.

'Many instances have I seen of nature's force and beneficence, exerted under numerous and formidable disadvantage, but none equal to that, with which you have been kind enough to present me. There is a pathos and delicacy in his serious poems; a vein of wit and humour in those of a more festive turn, which cannot be too much admired, nor too warmly approved; and I think I shall never open the book without feeling my astonishment renewed and increased. It was my wish to have expressed my approbation in verse; but whether from declining life or a temporary depression of spirits, it is at present out of my power to accomplish that agreeable intention.

'Mr Stewart, professor of morals in this university, had formerly read me three of the poems and I had desired to get my name inserted among the subscribers; but whether this was done or not I never could learn. I have little intercourse with Dr Blair, but will take care to have the poems communicated to him by the intervention of some mutual friend. It has been told me by a gentleman, to whom I showed the performances, and who sought a copy with diligence and ardour, that the whole

56

impression is already exhausted. It were therefore much to be wished, for the sake of the young man, that a second edition, more numerous than the former, could immediately be printed; as it appears certain that its intrinsic merit, and the exertion of the author's friends, might give it a more universal circulation than any thing of the kind which has been published within my memory.'

The critic's point about the possibility of a second edition must have caused Burns some anguish because the printer of the first edition, John Wilson of Kilmarnock, was reluctant to accept the risk unless the author was willing to pay for the paper needed to print an edition of one thousand. His caution may have been justified as far as sales in the neighbourhood were concerned, but Burns possibly began to think that Edinburgh held greater opportunities, particularly since this would help to alleviate the problems arising out of his love life.

At any rate, on 15 November 1786 he wrote to a friend, 'I am thinking to go to Edinburgh in a week or two at farthest to throw off a second impression of my book....' His decision may have been confirmed by the appearance in the October 1789 edition of the *Edinburgh Magazine* of a review of the poems which Burns could only consider favourable although it observed that the poet did not have 'the doric simplicity of Ramsay, or the brilliant imagination of Fergusson'. Anyway it continued, 'To those who admire the creations of untutored farmers and are blind to many faults for the sake of numberless beauties, his poems will yield singular gratification. His observations on human characters are acute and sagacious, and his descriptions are lively and just. Of rustic pleasantry he has a rich fund, and some of his softer scenes are touched with inimitable delicacy. . . .'

He set out for the capital on a borrowed pony, on Sunday, 27 November 1786, knowing that if his journey failed he could

57

still catch the *Roselle* which was due to sail, for Savannah, from Leith on 17 December. The journey took him two days and seems to have taken the form of a triumphal procession. Burns broke his journey at Covington Mains, near Biggar, in Lanarkshire, where he was entertained by a Mr Prentice who signalled his guest's arrival to the neighbouring farmers by hanging a sheet on a pitchfork. The ensuing celebration was so lavish in both wine and food, and lasted until so late in the morning, that the poet must have been exhausted as his pony pushed its way through the crowded streets to his lodging in Baxter's Close which he was to share (for a joint rent of three shillings a week) with John Richmond, an old friend of his from Mauchline, who was now a clerk in a law office.

The house he stayed in has long been demolished, although there is a tablet over the Lawnmarket entrance to Lady Stair's Close which states 'In a house on the east side of this close Robert Burns lived during his visit to Edinburgh, 1786.' Cunningham, in his *Life of Burns,* describes it as being a humble room with 'a deal table, a sanded floor and a chaff bed' although Hutton describes it as a fair-sized room, panelled with wood and looking out over Lady Stair's Close. It may be that he was shown the wrong room for a mercenary reason for he goes on to say, 'The house itself was an old house even in Burns's day, and now it is reduced to the very lowest social level. It holds no tablet to tell the passer-by of its former tenant; but nearly all of its present humble occupants are well aware, and very proud, of the fact that they sleep under the roof that once sheltered Robert Burns.'

His landlady was a staid, sober widow, disposed to piety and hating any skulduggery, who was sorely troubled by the prostitutes who had the rooms above the poet's. He wrote of her situation, 'She is at present in sore tribulation respecting some "Daughters of Belial" who are on the floor immediately

58

above . . . and as our floors are low and ill plaistered, we can easily distinguish our laughter-loving, night-rejoicing neighbours—when they are eating, when they are drinking, when they are singing, when they are etc.' Her religion was, however, a source of great strength and she told Burns that they should not be uneasy and envious because the wicked enjoy the good things of this life 'for these base jades who . . . lie up gandygoin with their filthy fellows, drinking the best of wines, and singing abominable songs, they shall one day lie in hell, weeping and wailing and gnashing their teeth over a cup of God's wrath'.

Burns spent his first few days in Edinburgh quietly, partly recovering from the extravagant hospitality he had received on his journey, but also spending his time in seeing the sights rather than in jollification. He viewed the Castle, gazed in the booksellers' windows, climbed Arthur's Seat and admired the ancient palace of Holyrood. He also visited his great literary forebears—standing bareheaded before Allan Ramsay's house, and the unmarked grave of Robert Fergusson.

The early days in a strange town were undoubtedly unsettling for the poet who must have worried about his reception and been unsure about his future. He had a letter of introduction to the Earl of Glencairn from James Dalrymple of Orangefield and one of his first actions was to present it. He also wrote a letter to Sir John Whitefoord, who had known of him in Mauchline and who happened to be in Edinburgh at the same time as Burns. The results of these letters must have flattered him excessively, for within a week of his arrival he was completely absorbed into the gay social whirl of the capital city. Ten days after his arrival he wrote back to Gavin Hamilton, in Ayrshire, perhaps with prescience rather than irony when we think of the countless Burns' Suppers celebrated round the world, 'For my own affairs, I am in a fair way of becoming as eminent as Thomas à Kempis, or John Bunyan; and you may expect henceforth to see my birthday inserted among the wonderful events, in the Poor Robin's and Aberdeen Almanacks, along with the black Monday, and the battle of Bothwell Bridge.—My Lord Glencairn and the Dean of the Faculty, Mr. H. Erskine, have taken me under their wing; and by all probability I shall soon be the tenth Worthy, and the Eighth Wise Man, of the world.'

Indeed Robert Burns had wasted little time and his patrons were unstinting in their efforts on his behalf. Glencairn was an ideal patron who welcomed him warmly on receipt of Dalrymple's letter. He was an amiable, good-looking man, as is recorded by Burns in his lines

> Bright as a cloudless summer sun
> With stately port he moves.

When we consider that the earl underwrote the second edition of the poems by taking a subscription of twenty-four copies, with his mother the Dowager Duchess, we can perhaps excuse the effusiveness with which Burns wrote of him that he 'looked so benevolently good at parting. God bless him! though I should never see him more, I shall love him until my dying day!' But the earl did not end his patronage by taking up part of the subscription himself, since he was a major influence in persuading the Caledonian Hunt to take up a hundred copies (thus earning the volume's dedication).

The other patron he mentions, Henry Erskine, was the second son of the Earl of Buchan and was related to Glencairn by marriage. He was the leading advocate, and the most famous Edinburgh wit, of his generation. He was also a leading liberal politician and was twice Lord Advocate. On the first of these occasions he succeeded Henry Dundas, then the 'uncrowned king of Scotland' as one of Pitt the Younger's lieutenants, who, when Erskine told him he was about to order the silk gown, suggested that 'for all the time you may want it, you had better borrow mine'. 'No doubt,' came the reply, 'your gown is made to fit any party, but it will never be said of Henry Erskine that he adopted the abandoned habits of his predecessor.' On another occasion he opened his address to the bench with 'I shall be brief, my Lords,' only to hear a grumbling voice from above, 'Hoots man, Harry, dinna be brief—dinna be brief'.

It was Erskine who, meeting Boswell leading Johnson through Parliament House, made his bow and conversed briefly with the famous visitor, only to press a shilling into Boswell's hand on leaving, being 'the common fee for a sight of wild beasts'.

Erskine admired Burns's poems and, because of his eminent position, was able to introduce him into society where the poet's great personal charm soon overcame any resistance to the 'ploughman poet'. His success was assured when he won the approval of the fourth Duke of Gordon and, perhaps even more important, of his beautiful and notorious wife.

She was one of the daughters of Lady Maxwell of Monreith and had spent her childhood in a close off the High Street where she and her sisters used to ride up and down gaily on the bare backs of the pigs which were kept under the fore stairs. One of the 'beautiful people' of the eighteenth century, of whom it was said 'she is never absent from a public place, and the later the hour, so much the better. It is often four o'clock in the morning before she goes to bed, and she never requires more than five hours' sleep. Dancing, cards and company occupy her whole time.' According to one story she had been faithful to her husband during the early years of her marriage but she decided to repay him in his own coin for his continual infidelities. The result was that, when a suitor for her daughter's hand was concerned about the well-known tendency to

61

insanity of the Gordon family, she was able to reassure him by admitting there was not a drop of Gordon blood in her daughter's veins. One of the leaders of fashion in London, as well as Edinburgh, to be accepted by her meant that Burns became the lion of the season. After all, had not the Duchess of Gordon declared that his conversation carried her off her feet as no other man's had ever done?

Shrewdly Burns adopted the role of 'ploughman poet'. He had first accepted this role in the introduction to the Kilmarnock Edition of his poems and he had presumably merely intended it as a trivial falsification which would aid the sales of his book. He was confirmed in it by the reviews of Sibbald and Mackenzie and tended to play upon this background in the *salons* of Edinburgh society. Later, admittedly, it did begin to affect his attitude towards his art but it was never a true picture of the man despite the myth which has now so enfolded the truth.

At this time Burns was twenty-eight years old, about five feet ten in height, and had a strong robust figure although he was slightly stooped in the shoulders from following the plough as a young man. His face would have belonged to a well-to-do farmer, or the captain of a merchantman, until his eyes flashed most brilliantly, glowing like fires in moments of excitement. With his hair lank and unpowdered, tied in a short queue at the back, dressed in a blue coat with metal buttons, buff waistcoat with broad blue stripes, tight buckskin breeches and jockey boots with yellow tops, and carrying a whip, the poet presented a dignified, but simple, appearance which carried him successfully through his many meetings with the social elite. But above all it was the charm of his conversation and the vitality of his genius which captured the hearts and minds of these men and women, both frivolous and learned.

Lockhart, in his *Life of Burns*, says: 'During the winter Burns continued to lodge with John Richmond, and we have the authority of this early friend of the poet for the statement that while he did so "he kept good hours". He removed afterwards to the house of Mr Nicoll (one of the teachers of the High School of Edinburgh), on the Buccleuch Road; and this change is, I suppose, to be considered a symptom that the keeping of good hours was beginning to be irksome.... With a warm heart the man united a fierce, irascible temper, a scorn of many of the decencies of life, a noisy contempt of religion, at least of the religious institutions of his country, and a violent propensity for the bottle.' The Buccleuch Road is now called Buccleuch Street and William Nicoll's house was over the pend leading into St Patrick Square, directly opposite Buccleuch Place; his flat was on the top floor. If Burns did not lodge with Nicoll, he was certainly familiar with the neighbourhood, for in the archway there used to be a hole-in-the-wall, still in existence in the eighteen-nineties, which led to an underground public house kept by Lucky Pringle which was much frequented by both Nicoll and Burns. For Nicoll was one of Burns's boon companions, indeed he is the eponymous hero of 'Willie brew'd a peck o' maut' which celebrates an evening spent carousing in Moffat.

O Willie brew'd a peck o' maut,
    And Rob and Allan cam to pree;
Three blyther hearts, that lee-lang night,
    Ye wid na found in Christendie.

We are na fou, we're nae that fou,
    But jist a drappie in our e'e;
The cock may craw, the day may daw,
    And ay we'll taste the barley bree.

This change of residence may mark some dissatisfaction with the drawing-rooms of the aristocracy and the well-meant,

63

but frequently inapposite, criticism of the literati. Burns met Henry Mackenzie, Hugh Blair and Dugald Stewart but, although they recognized his talent, they wanted to force him into the mould of Scotland's national poet, which meant writing in English. Clearly these people were not his natural congeners. At first he had been accepted, as has happened to many another artist, as 'the latest rage', an amusing 'must' for a successful party. Burns never took kindly to this attitude and when a peeress asked him to an assembly without the formality of an introduction he was so angered at being treated as an object for exhibition that he agreed to attend but only if she would invite the Learned Pig from its booth in the Grassmarket as well. During this period he wrote to a friend, 'I am willing to believe that my abilities deserved a better fate than the veriest shades of life; but to be dragged forth, with all my imperfections on my head, to the full glare of learned and polite observation is what, I am afraid, I shall have bitter reason to repent.'

At least the visit had been successful in its primary aim, for Glencairn had introduced Burns to William Creech, the foremost bookseller and publisher in Edinburgh of that time. Creech's shop was at the foot of the Luckenbooths below the premises formerly occupied by Allan Ramsay and, as in his day, the literary gentlemen met there regularly. Creech, in turn, introduced Burns to William Smellie who became the printer of the second, and third, editions—but let it be remembered, always at the poet's own risk, for he had to pay both the printer and the binder. Smellie quickly introduced his new friend to the world of club life of which he was a leading member. Fergusson's favourite, the Cape Club, was still flourishing at this time and he may have paid it a visit out of sentiment but the society he found most to his taste, and most relaxing after spending the afternoons avoiding 'more success-

64

fully than most Scotchmen the peculiarities of Scottish phraseology', was that of the Crochallan Fencibles who met in the tavern belonging to Dawney Douglas in Anchor Close. The name comes in part from derision for the volunteer corps of militia which was then being raised in the city and in part from the landlord's favourite song—'Crodh Chailein' (Colin's Cattle). This is a mournful Gaelic air about a man whose wife dies young but returns as a shimmering ghost to tend her husband's cattle.

Not that all their songs were of this character, for drinking was one of their main reasons for meeting—the other being bawdry, both in talk and song. One result of their riotous evenings was Burns's magnificent collection of bawdy lyrics which has been published as *The Merry Muses of Caledonia.** Burns drew on his knowledge of Scottish folk song in creating this book but he added verses of his own and polished the remainder. According to tradition the manuscript for this book vanished from Burns's home on the evening of his death only to reappear, published anonymously, before 1800. The present-day editions are based on the sole copy of this edition to escape the destroying puritanism of the Victorians.

This was not the only collection of verse to come out of those hard-drinking evenings, however, since Burns met among the Fencibles the music engraver, James Johnson, who was just completing the first volume of his *Scots Musical Museum.* This ambitious project would have quickly foundered but for Burns's talent, both as a poet himself and as an enthusiast for the tradition of folk poetry in Scotland.

Tales of the conviviality of these evenings soon began to circulate among the drawing-rooms of Edinburgh. Henry Mackenzie, admittedly writing years later, may be taken to represent the typical reaction of the middle class literati of the

*Available as a paperback published by Luxor Press.

65

capital: 'alas! it was the Patronage and Companionship which Burns obtained, that changed the Colour of his later life; the patronage of dissipated men of high rank, and the Companionship of clever and witty, but dissipated men of lower rank. The notice of the former flattered his vanity . . . but the levity of both his Patrons and his associates Dwelt on the Surface of his Mind, and prompted some of his Poetry which offended the serious, and lost him better friends than those which that poetry had acquired.' Dugald Stewart, although admitting that he had never seen the poet drunk (and quoting Burns as saying that 'the weakness of his stomach was such as to deprive him entirely of any merit in his temperance') is reported to have said that 'his Conduct and Manners had become so degraded that decent persons could hardly take any notice of him'.

How much of this attitude stemmed from Burns's social activities and how much from his persistence in writing in the vernacular, is an open question. Undoubtedly the salons of Edinburgh were willing to welcome him as a national poet and Mackenzie and his friends were only too willing to greet effusively poems like 'Edina! Scotia's darling seat' because they are written in English, even though they are so much weaker than a poem on the same subject like 'Auld Reekie' by Robert Fergusson:

Auld Reekie! thou'rt a canty hole
A bield for mony a cauldrife soul
Wha' snugly at thine ingle loll
   Baith warm and couth,
While round they gar the bicker roll
   To weet their mouth.

As one of these critics said to Burns, of his use of the 'provincial dialect', 'Why should you, by using *that*, limit the number of your admirers to those who understand the Scottish, when you can extend it to all persons of taste who understand the English language?'

The publication of the first Edinburgh edition was so heavily oversubscribed that a second and even a third edition were called for until Burns had printed three thousand copies of his book. Creech, the bookseller, quickly realized the profits that could be made from this unexpected best-seller and he purchased—or thought he purchased—the copyright of the poems for one hundred guineas, a figure suggested by Henry Mackenzie. This agreement was to lead to much bitter quarrelling between the poet and the publisher over the next year.

As was only to be expected, the publication of the book was met with some hostile criticism because of the 'licentiousness' of some of the poems—'It must be allowed that there are exceptionable parts of the volume he has given to the public, which custom would have suppressed or correction struck out; but Poets are seldom critics, and our Poet had, alas! no friends or companions from whom correction could be obtained. When we reflect on his rank in life, and the habits to which he must have been subject, and the society in which he must have mixed, we regret perhaps more than wonder, that delicacy should be so offended in perusing a volume in which there is so much to interest and please us.'

Thus ended Burns's first winter in Edinburgh, in which he had passed from being a novelty, welcome in all the best drawing-rooms, to being an embarrassment both because of the company he kept and his outspoken attitude towards his superiors. His poems had been published successfully and now, when people were perhaps beginning to ignore him, or greeting him with less warmth than previously, he could relax by touring through the Borders with some of the hard-drinking, woman-chasing, boon companions he had made during his short stay. When he returned to Edinburgh for his second winter, he lodged with William Cruikshank, like William Nicoll a schoolmaster at the High School, in a house on the south-west corner of St James's Square, in the New Town. From here he worked on the production of the second volume of the *Scots Musical Museum* which, besides many songs collected by Burns and his friends, also contains many songs written by him. He was also pursuing his quest for permanent employment and attempting to settle the financial position with Creech.

While Burns knew much about farming, his scope outside this area was strictly limited and the only practical possibility was in the Excise. He had thought of this as early as 1786 but did not pursue it very seriously until during this second visit to the capital. Perhaps it was in following this idea that he went to tea with a revenue officer, John Nimmo, on 6 December 1788. At that tea his hostess introduced him to a Mrs James Maclehose who was to become famous as Clarinda.

Mrs Maclehose had just turned twenty-nine when this meeting, for which she had worked tirelessly, occurred. She was a grass-widow who lived with her two children in a tiny flat off Potterrow and considered herself to have been hard done by in her short life. Her naturally voluptuous figure, her 'spaniel' eyes framed with fluttering lashes, and her poetic pretensions had attracted a young ne'er do well Glaswegian law agent who had married her at the age of eighteen, against her father's wishes, presented her with three children in the next four years and then departed for Jamaica after his family had refused to pay his debts any longer. Nancy had moved to Edinburgh with her children in pursuit of the 'culture' of which she, like so many ardent amateurs, 'knew' she was one of the leaders. To a certain extent, therefore, her interest in meeting Burns must have been because his poetry was gaining such a reputation among 'society' in Edinburgh but her frustrations must have excited her interest in a man who was generally credited with a flair for love-making. Whatever her reasons, Mrs Maclehose went home from this first meeting and invited the poet to have tea with her at eight o'clock on the following Thursday evening.

Thursday was to bring disappointment. 'I had set no small store by my tea-drinking tonight, and have not often been so disappointed. Saturday evening I shall embrace the opportunity with the greatest pleasure.' But he also introduced some very typical flattery: 'I must ever regret that I so lately got an acquaintance I shall ever highly esteem, and in whose welfare I shall ever be warmly interested.'

Opinions differ over the next event. One biographer has written about it that 'Fate held up her finger in warning', while another has it that 'the Devil, seeing his opportunity, stepped in'—but let Burns tell it himself, in a rather warmer note than his first: 'I can say with truth, Madam, that I never met with a person in my life whom I more anxiously wished to meet again than yourself. Tonight I was to have had that great pleasure—I was intoxicated with the idea—but an unlucky fall from a coach has so bruised one of my knees, that I can't stir my leg off the cushion. So, if I don't see you again, I shall not rest in my grave for chagrin. I was vexed to the soul I had not seen you sooner; I determined to cultivate your friendship with the enthusiasm of Religion; but thus has Fortune ever served me. I cannot bear the thought of leaving Edinburgh without seeing you—I know not how I am to account for it—I am so strangely taken with some people; nor am I often mistaken. You are a stranger to me; but I am an odd being: some yet unnamed feelings, things not principles, but better than whims, carry me farther than boasted reason ever did a Philosopher. Farewell! every happiness be yours!' Obviously Nancy's charms had gained markedly in Burns's fertile imagination.

69

He was quick to pursue the line of literary flattery following the receipt of some verses which began

> When first you saw *Clarinda's* charms
> What rapture in your bosom grew!
> Her heart was shut to Love's alarms,
> But then—you'd nothing else to do.

and adopted the idea of using Arcadian names for their poetic correspondence, taking the name of *Sylvander*. He referred to her fine taste and turn for 'poesy' and said that her verse was 'worthy of Sappho', although this may be mere poetic exaggeration.

His letters became more passionate—'I believe there is no holding converse with an amiable woman, much less a gloriously amiable fine woman, without some mixture of that delicious Passion, whose most devoted Slave I have more than once had the honour of being.' But his darling Clarinda was a little frightened by the violence of his approach. In letter after letter she tries to moderate his comments—thinking perhaps of the attitude that would be adopted by her puritanical relations, upon whom she relied for money, if her extra-marital affair became public knowledge—but, because she was truly attracted to him, she had to keep his love without yielding her body. On the other hand, Burns was head over heels in love and in a letter to an old friend he wrote: 'Almighty Love still "reigns and revels" in my bosom; and I am at this moment ready to hang myself for a young Edinburgh widow'—even he felt the need to shade the truth slightly about the absent husband.

Indeed his passion was so strong that it overcame the handicap of his bruised knee and, hirpling but happy, he hasted round to his Clarinda in a sedan chair. He found her with a headache but the meeting, which lasted for an hour, confirmed the strength of his attachment—and hers. After this she lived between meetings, at least on paper, only by hoping to catch a glimpse of the loved one as she passed the poet's window in St James's Square. It was from here that Burns wrote: 'I am certain I saw you, Clarinda, but you don't look to the proper storey for a poet's lodging—"where speculation roosted near the sky". I could almost have thrown myself over for very vexation. Why didn't you look higher? It has spoiled my peace for the day. To be so near my charming Clarinda—to miss her look when it was searching for me! . . . I am sure the soul is capable of disease for mine has convulsed itself into an inflammatory fever.' Certainly, Burns was unable to sleep at night and ends several letters with wishes for a good night's rest. Clarinda was also losing sleep—in her case because of the illness of one of her children.

The damage had been done, however, and the affair between the 'ploughman poet' and the 'lady of fashion' was beginning to creep into the talk of the respectable. Clarinda received letters from the minister of her kirk and from her uncle, Lord Craig, reprimanding her for her 'dissolute' behaviour. Burns dismissed the former as 'damned sophistry' and declared that 'the half-inch soul of an unfeeling, cold-blooded, pitiful Presbyterian bigot cannot forgive anything above his dungeon-bosom and foggy head'.

Burns had, however, managed to secure the money Creech owed him and had nothing else to hold him in Edinburgh. So on 18 February 1789 he rode out of the city to return home—having assured his sweetheart of his love and a steady flow of letters. A few letters did come but they gradually diminished in passion until they ceased and, at last, the poet descended to toasting his former 'meridian sun' as 'Mrs Mack'.

Not that all the inhabitants of Edinburgh felt great sympathy for Mrs Maclehose. One such, when pointing out the poet's

71

window in St James's Square—as it had been pointed out to him by Clarinda herself—reminisced about the lady in her old age when she lived beneath his father in a small flat in a house at Greenside, on an insignificant annuity allowed her by her brother. She never wearied of telling the story of her flirtation with Burns and, as he remarked, 'The auld donnert leddy bodie spoke o' her love for the poet just like a hellicat bit lassie in her teens, and while exhibitin' to her cronies the faded letters from her Robbie she would just greet like a bairn. Puir auld creature, she never till the moment o' her death jaloused or dooted Robbie's professed love for her; but, sir, you ken he was juist makin' a fule o' her, as his letters amply show.'

There may be some truth in this suggestion for, on his free evenings, Burns was still indulging in the congenial company of the clubmen and the Freemasons. This latter association went back to his first visit when, on 14 January 1787, Burns wrote: 'I went to a Mason Lodge yesternight, where the M.W. Grand Master Charteris and all the Grand Lodge of Scotland visited. The meeting was numerous and elegant; all the different lodges about town were present in all their pomp. The Grand Master, who presided with all solemnity, among other general toasts gave 'Caledonia and Caledonia's Bard, Brother B——,' which rang through the whole assembly with multiplied honours and repeated acclamation. As I had no idea such a thing would happen I was downright thunderstruck, and, trembling in every nerve, made the best return in my power.'

This was at the Canongate Kilwinning Lodge of Freemasons, of which Burns afterwards was made poet laureate; and his inauguration, painted by William Stewart Watson, is very familiar because of the many engravings made of it. The hall of the Kilwinning Lodge is still standing on the west side of St John Street, just off the Canongate. It is a square, rigid, and

72

rather grim building in which the Lodge still meets and where they keep their quaint and curious records.

Also dating from his first visit to Edinburgh is Burns's sole meeting with Walter Scott who was to become the natural heir early in the following century. Scott, writing to his biographer Lockhart, described this meeting, in one of the best pieces of his prose, in the following terms: 'As for Burns I may truly say, *Virgilium vidi tantum.* I was a lad of fifteen in 1786–87, when he came first to Edinburgh, but had sense and feeling enough to be much interested in his poetry, and would have given the world to know him; but I had very little acquaintance with any literary people, and still less with the gentry of the West Country, the two sets that he most frequented. Mr Thomas Grierson was at that time a clerk of my father's. He knew Burns, and promised to ask him to his lodgings to dinner, but had no opportunity to keep his word, otherwise I might have seen more of this distinguished man. As it was, I saw him one day at the late venerable Professor Ferguson's, where there were several gentlemen of literary reputation, among whom I remember the celebrated Dr Dugald Stewart. Of course we youngsters sat silent, looked and listened. The only thing I remember which was remarkable in Burns' manner was the effect produced upon him by a print of Bunbury's representing a soldier lying dead on the snow, his dog sitting in misery on the one side, on the other his widow, with a child in her arms. These lines were written beneath:

Cold on Canadian hills or Minden's plain,
    Perhaps that parent wept her soldier slain;
Bent o'er her babe, her eye dissolved in dew;
    The big drops, mingling with the milk he drew,
Gave the sad presage of his future years,
    The child of misery, baptized in tears.

'Burns seemed much affected by the print, or rather the ideas which it suggested to his mind. He actually shed tears. He asked whose the lines were, and it chanced that nobody but myself remembered that they occur in a half-forgotten poem of Langhorne's called by the unpromising title of 'The Justice of the Peace'. I whispered my information to a friend present, who mentioned it to Burns, who rewarded me with a look and a word which, though of mere civility, I then received and still recollect with very great pleasure.

'His person was strong and robust; his manners rustic, not clownish; a sort of dignified plainness and simplicity, which received part of its effect perhaps from one's knowledge of his extraordinary talents. His features are represented in Mr Nasmyth's picture, but to me it conveys the idea that they are diminished as if seen in perspective. I think his countenance was more massive than it looks in any of the portraits. I would have taken the poet, had I not known what he was, for a very sagacious country farmer of the old Scottish school—i.e., none of your modern agriculturists who keep labourers for their drudgery, but the douce gudeman who held his own plough. There was a strong expression of sense and shrewdness in all his lineaments; the eye alone, I think, indicated the poetical character and temperament. It was large and of a dark cast, and glowed (I say literally glowed) when he spoke with feeling or interest. I never saw such another eye in a human head, though I have seen the most distinguished men of my time. His conversation expressed perfect self-confidence, without the slightest presumption. Among the men who were the most learned of their time and country, he expressed himself with perfect firmness, but without the least intrusive forwardness; and when he differed in opinion he did not hesitate to express it firmly, yet at the same time with modesty. I do not remember any of his conversation distinctly enough to be quoted, nor did

I ever see him again, except in the street, where he did not recognize me, as I could not expect he should.'

The story is familiar to all admirers of both the writers, but the question of exactly which house in Edinburgh was their meeting-place seems to have been the subject of much learned discussion. The problem seems to have been finally resolved and a small tablet on Sciennes (pronounced *sheens*) Hill House commemorates the glorious moment in Scottish literature. The house, standing in Braid Place, is now the Royal Hospital for Sick Children but, in its day, it must have been a most imposing mansion. The present front, extensively rebuilt, was the back of the house lived in by Adam Ferguson, of which the original front still remains in part. It was four windows wide and three storeys high; on its roof is a balustrade upon which can still be seen the groups of flowers and fruit carved on it when it was first built.

Sciennes Hill House is only one of the many buildings associated with the 'Magician of the North' which still survive in contemporary Edinburgh. However, his birthplace was demolished to make room for the expansion of the university in the nineteenth century.

The 'Magician', Walter Scott, was born on 15 August 1771 in a house at the top of College Wynd which led, in those days, from the Cowgate to the college buildings and was described by a native as 'a steep and straightened alley'. Originally called the Wynd of the Blessed Virgin-in-the-Fields the tall house which stood at its head was built on the site of Kirk-o'-Field which was blown up to murder Darnley in February 1567. The Scotts' flat was typical of the late eighteenth century—in a house standing in the corner of a small court, at the top of a common stair covered in filth, with windows looking out on rotting refuse in which pigs and children played indiscriminately. There can be little wonder that six of the eight children

75

his mother bore died in infancy All that now remains to remind us of those days is a small tablet on the wall of 8 Chambers Street which tells us that the birthplace was 'near this spot' and the bit of College Wynd which now makes Guthrie Street.

It was undoubtedly with some thanksgiving that the family moved to the airy pleasantness of the new-built George Square. Erected by the architect James Brown (and named by him after his brother George—the truckling to royalty by using their names for public places did not begin until George III insisted that Princes Street be called after his son) in what was virtually open country, it soon became the centre of fashion. To this day it is still an exquisite example of Scottish eighteenth-century architecture and its houses are much better designed than most of those in the New Town, although it must be admitted that most of the other houses were built by more commercial architects than James Brown.

It was in this house, 25 George Square, that Walter Scott spent most of his early years and it was here that Mrs Alicia Cockburn, the author of *The Flowers of the Forest*, found 'the most extraordinary genius of a boy I ever saw. He was reading a poem to his mother when I went in. I made him read on; it was the description of a shipwreck. His passion rose with the storm. "There's the mast gone," says he. "Crash it goes! They will all perish!" After his agitation he turns to me. "That is too melancholy," says he, "I had better read you something more amusing." I proposed a little chat and asked his opinion of Milton and other books he was reading, which he gave me wonderfully. . . . When taken to bed last night, he told his aunt he liked that lady. "What lady?" says she. "Why, Mrs Cockburn, for I think she is a virtuoso, like myself." "Dear Walter," says Aunt Jenny, "what is a virtuoso?" "Don't you know? Why, it's one that wishes and will know everything.". . . Pray, what age do you suppose that boy to be? Name it now, before I tell you.

76

Why twelve or fourteen. No such thing; he is not quite six years old.'

It was in this house, too, that Scott and his brothers received their early education from a tutor and it is said that their neighbour, Lady Cumming, sent round one day 'to beg that all the boys might not be flogged at the same hour. Though she had no doubt the punishment was well deserved, the noise was dreadful.' How much of this punishment came Scott's way was probably minimal, and he remembered his early years for the evenings spent reading Shakespear's plays by the fire in his mother's dressing room until the sound of the family moving from their supper below gave him notice that it was time to return to his own bed.

Scott's first school was 'in a small cottage-like building with a red-tiled roof, in Hamilton's Entry, off Bristo Street', but the experiment did not last long and he learned the first stages of Latin from a private tutor. In October 1779 he went to the High School—not the present building at the foot of Calton Hill but the second school which was opened in 1777. The building still survives as the Old Infirmary, in the High School Yards, but it is now occupied by some of the departments of the University. There he came under the influence of the great Dr Alexander Adam, whose portrait by Raeburn is surely one of that artist's great productions. Dr Adam was extremely proud of his own abilities and would say to new boys, 'Come away, sir, you will see more here in an hour than you will in any other school in Europe.' He had many other eminent pupils as well as Scott, including Jeffrey and Horner, and his complete identification with the scholastic life may be seen in his dying utterance, 'Boys, it is growing dark, you may go home.'

The young Scott early showed every sign of his later genius as a writer but just as much of his education occurred in 'the Yards', or playground, as in the classroom. Although he had

77

suffered an attack of infantile paralysis while still a baby he was determined that the resultant lameness would be no bar to his physical activity. He was indeed always fighting and climbing—manning 'the Cowgate Port' in the winter snowball fights, scrambling over the Salisbury Crags, leading his schoolmates in the bickers with the street urchins (in which the weapons used were stones—broken heads were a frequent result), or climbing the 'kittle nine stanes' on the Castle Rock.

One story of his schoolboy activities was told by himself in later years. 'There was a boy in my class at school who stood always at the top, nor could I with all my efforts supplant him. Day came after day and still he kept his place, do what I would, till at length I observed that when a question was asked him he always fumbled with his fingers at a particular button in the lower part of his waistcoat. To remove it, therefore, became expedient in my eyes, and in an evil moment it was removed with a knife. Great was my anxiety to know the success of my measure; and it succeeded too well. When the boy was again questioned, his fingers sought again for the button, but it was not to be found. In his distress he looked down for it; it was to be seen no more than to be felt. He stood confounded, and I took possession of his place; nor did he ever recover it, or ever, I believe, suspect who was the author of his wrong. Often in after life has the sight of him smote me as I passed by him; and often have I resolved to make him some reparation; but it ended in good resolutions. Though I never renewed my acquaintance with him, I often saw him, for he filled some inferior office in one of the courts of law at Edinburgh. Poor fellow! I believe he is dead. He took early to drinking.'

Apart from this type of activity Scott was also making a name for himself at school as a storyteller. In an autobiographical fragment he wrote: 'In the winter play hours, when hard exercise was impossible, my tales used to assemble an admiring

78

audience round Lucky Brown's fireside, and happy was he that could sit next to the inexhaustible narrator.' He only stayed at the High School for four years and left in 1783 to go to the university. 'I left the High School . . . with a great quantity of general information, ill arranged, indeed, and collected without system, yet deeply impressed upon my mind; readily assorted by my power of connection and memory, and gilded, if I may be permitted to say so, by a vivid and active imagination.'

The buildings of the University known to Scott were still the original ones of the foundation and were widely recognized as being a disgrace to the capital of Scotland. They were not to be replaced, however, until 1789, after Scott had left the College, and it is these buildings which now form the Old Quad.

Going to University at the age of twelve was quite common in eighteenth-century Edinburgh and the lectures were very similar to the classes at the High School. Indeed most students did not qualify for a degree but simply attended the classes in those subjects which they felt would benefit them most. Scott went to several courses, but forgot as much as he learned, and left in 1786, after a serious illness, to be indentured for five years as his father's apprentice and to study the law. He afterwards confessed, 'The drudgery of the office I disliked, and the confinement I altogether detested; but I loved my father, and I felt the natural pride and pleasure of rendering myself useful to him. I was ambitious also; and among my companions in labour the only way to gratify ambition was to labour hard and well.'

The rigours of the law did not prevent him pursuing his more physical activities—he could walk thirty miles in a day and ride a horse as long as it could carry him. He was a roaring boy, a desperate climber, a deep drinker, and a stout player at singlestick. According to one story he defended himself with

79

his stick against three attackers for an hour by the Tron clock. He was a tall, broad-shouldered youth with a very deep chest and arms like a blacksmith's. One of his feats was to lift an anvil by the horn, and James Hogg thought Scott was the strongest man he knew. And his temper was always near the surface. As a naval officer said after meeting him, 'Though you may think him a poor lamiter, he's the first to begin a row, and the last to end it.'

In 1792 Scott passed his final examinations and qualified as an advocate and for the next few years walked the floor of Parliament House waiting to be hired, and maintaining his reputation as a story-teller. He was especially famous for his impersonation of Lord Eskgrove, who was grotesque and, though alleged to be very learned, certainly possessed a unique mode of expression. Accurate law reports also began at this time and Eskgrove's alarmed 'He taks doun ma very words' can easily be understood.

Eskgrove once requested a female witness to 'Lift up your veil, throw off all modesty and look me in the face,' and he would tell the jury, 'And so, gentlemen, having shown you the pannell's argument is utterly impossible I shall now proceed to show you that it is extremely improbabill.' When condemning a prisoner to death, he frequently added: 'Whatever your religi-ous persua-shon may be, or even if, as I suppose, you be of no persua-shon at all, there are plenty of rever-end gentlemen who will be most happy for to show you the way to yeternal life.'

Eskgrove was particularly noted for his keen understanding of just where a criminal act achieved true enormity. Sentencing some thieves he explained their crimes—assault, robbery, hamesucken—most elaborately, giving etymologies where necessary, and ended with the climactic, 'All this you did; and God preserve us! Joost when they were sitten doun to their denner.' On another occasion he passed sentence on a tailor for stabbing a soldier and, in endeavouring to show the poor man where he had erred, said, 'And not only did you murder him, whereby he was berea-ved of his life, but you did thrust, or push, or pierce, or project, or propell, the le-thall weapon through the belly-band of his regimen-tal breeches, which were his Majes-ty's!'

Not all Scott's time was spent in the Outer House and he was busy collecting ballads and soldiering with the Royal Edinburgh Volunteer Light Dragoons. Years later the Tsar of Russia met him in Paris, in uniform, and asked which battles he had been engaged in, only to receive the reply 'some slight actions, such as the battle of the Cross Causeway and the affair of Moredoun Mill'. These activities did not prevent him leading the normal life of a young man, and one young lady, who imparts a slight rose-colour to her description, wrote: 'His eyes were clear, open and well set, with a changeful radiance, to which teeth of the most perfect regularity and whiteness lent their assistance, while the noble expanse and elevation of his brow gave to the whole aspect a dignity far above the charm of mere features. His smile was always delightful, and I can easily fancy the peculiar intermixture of tenderness and gravity, with playful innocent hilarity and humour in the expression, as being well calculated to fix a fair lady's eye.'

With such an appearance he could not escape a romantic adventure and one wet Sunday while he was still in his teens he offered his umbrella to a girl of only fifteen outside Greyfriars Church, and had his first sight of the face that was to haunt his dreams for many years after. She was the daughter of Sir John and Lady Jane Stuart-Belsches and was not only well-born, being related on her mother's side to the Earl of Leven and Melville, but was also going to inherit a considerable fortune. Her portrait, which shows large blue eyes set in peaches and

81

cream and framed by dark brown ringlets, explains the poet's ardour and also his disappointment when, after many years of hoping and talking, the 'Lady of the Green Mantle' rejected him and married the banker, William Forbes of Pitsligo, who had been one of Scott's friends at college and a volunteer.

The wound went deep and thirty-five years later he sat on a gravestone near where he had cut her name in the turf at the castle gate of St Andrew's and wondered why it 'should still aggitate my heart'. He met her again in Edinburgh when she was middle-aged, and her daughter had been dead for many years, and the cold ashes glowed once more. 'I fairly softened myself, like an old fool, with recalling stories, till I was fit for nothing but shedding tears and repeating verses for the whole night. This is sad work. The very grave gives up its dead, and time rolls back thirty years to add to my perplexities.'

In July 1797 he went on a journey to the Lake District and met, and fell in love with, Charlotte Carpenter, and immediately proposed marriage. How far this was just a rebound from his earlier disappointment is debatable but Scott wrote twelve years later, 'Mrs Scott's match and mine was of our own making and proceeded from the most sincere affection on both sides, which has rather increased than diminished during twelve years' marriage. But it was something short of love in all its forms, which I suspect people only feel once in all their lives; folk who have been nearly drowned in bathing rarely venturing a second time out of their depth.'

The young couple were married on Christmas Eve 1797 and made their first house together in lodgings on the second floor of 108 George Street, in a house which is still standing, next door to the corner of Castle Street. This accommodation was only temporary, for they soon moved to 10 South Castle Street but only stayed for a few months until, later in 1798, they moved to the house that they were to occupy for the next twenty-eight years, and where most of the Waverley novels were to be written.

This house, 39 Castle Street, is easily identified since a bust of Sir Walter can be seen through the fanlight above the door, and there is an inscription on the front of the house as well. The author's study was at the back and had 'a single Venetian window opening on a patch of turf not much larger than itself and the aspect of the place was sombrous. . . . The only table was a massive piece of furniture which he had constructed on the model of one at Rokeby, with a desk and all its appurtenances on either side that an amanuensis might work opposite to him when he chose. . . . His own writing apparatus was a very handsome old box richly carved, and lined with crimson velvet. . . . The room had no place for pictures, except one, an original portrait of Claverhouse, which hung over the chimney-piece with a Highland target on either side, and broadswords and dirks (each having its own story) dispersed star fashion round them.'

This was the house where Scott lived at the height of his fame and prosperity and he left it, after the financial crash in 1826, with no little regret, as he noted in his journal: 'March 15—This morning I leave No. 39 Castle Street, for the last time . . . In all my former changes of residence it was from good to better; this is retrograding. I leave this house for sale, and I cease to be an Edinburgh citizen, in the sense of being a proprietor, which my father and I have been for sixty years at least. So farewell, poor 39.' It is interesting to note that, when Captain Basil Hall visited the house five months after Scott's departure, he had to write of it, 'In the days of his good-luck he used to live at No. 39 North Castle Street, in a house befitting a rich baronet; but on reaching the door I found the plate on it covered with rust (so soon is glory obscured), the windows shuttered up, dirty and comfortless; and from the side of me projected a board "To Sell". The stairs were unwashed, and not a footmark told of the ancient hospitality which reigned within. In all nations with which I am acquainted, the fashionable world moves westwards, in imitation, perhaps, of the greater tide of civilization; and *vice versa*, those persons who decline in fortune, which is mostly equivalent to declining in fashion, shape their course eastward. Accordingly, by an involuntary impulse, I turned my head that way, and, inquiring at the Clubs in Princes Street, learned that he now resided in St David Street, No. 6.'

Scott had left his house at Abbotsford because he had to return to Edinburgh to attend to his duties at the court and had rented these shabby, bug-infested lodgings. Four days after his arrival he was followed by the news from home that his wife was dead. Captain Basil Hall visited him soon after this and has left the following description. 'I was rather glad to recognize my old friend the Abbotsford butler, who answered the door. . . . At the top of the stairs we saw a small tray, with a single plate and glasses for a solitary person's dinner. . . . As he rose to receive us, he closed the volume which he had been extracting from, and came forward to shake hands. He was, of course, in deep mourning, with weepers, and the other trappings of woe, but his countenance, though certainly a little woe-begone was not cut into any very deep furrows. . . . After sitting a quarter of an hour we came away, well pleased to see our friend quite unbroken in spirit, and though bowed down a little by the blast, and here and there a branch the less, as sturdy in the trunk as ever.'

Scott himself wrote, on moving in to Mrs Brown's house, 'Well, here I am in Arden. And I may say with Touchstone, "When I was at home I was in a better place," I must, when there is occasion, draw to my own Bailie Nicol Jarvie's consolation, "One cannot carry the comforts of the Saut Market about

84

with one." Were I at ease in my mind, I think the body is very well cared for.' He lived in this second-rate lodging house until 13 July 1826 and began work upon his *Napoleon* here. On his return to the city in November he took a furnished house at 3 Walker Street, which was much more comfortable in every way. It was from this house that he walked, on the evening of 23 February 1827, to the Assembly Rooms in George Street to attend the Theatrical Fund Dinner at which he confessed for the first time in public to the authorship of the 'Waverley Novels'. Although this had long been an open secret the sensation produced by this announcement was, in Lockhart's phrase, 'unprecedented'.

Between the years 1828 and 1830 Scott lived at 6 Shandwick Place but nothing now remains of the house. It was in this house that on 15 February 1830 Scott was stricken with paralysis after his return from Parliament House at two o'clock in the afternoon. He remained speechless for about ten minutes by which time a surgeon had arrived and bled him. He gradually recovered his possession of speech and of all his faculties, so that when he went out again after a short interval, most people observed no serious change—though his friends noticed a slight nervous twist of the mouth and a slight stammer. Scott knew death was near and wrote resignedly, 'It looks woundy like palsy or apoplexy. Well, be it what it will, I can stand it.'

He refused to reduce his rate of working, however, but, even here, the tide was running out. He retired from the court later in the same year and went to live at Abbotsford, thinking that by the end of 1832 he would be clear of all his debts. He made a few visits to Edinburgh—in February 1831, for example, when he was the guest of his publisher, Robert Cadell, at 16 Atholl Crescent, where he executed his last will. He spent his last two nights in Edinburgh at the Douglas Hotel, 34 and 35 St

Andrew Square, now the head office of the Scottish Union and National Insurance Company. He was brought there, ill and dying, on his return from Italy in 1832 and, on the morning of 11 July he was carried unconscious from this house and from Edinburgh, to die at Abbotsford two months later.

To follow the footsteps of Sir Walter Scott in Edinburgh it is only necessary to walk through all the streets and alleys of the Old Town, and through most of the streets and avenues of the New. Despite his fondness for Abbotsford, he was a thorough townsman at heart, and he knew and loved every inch of the smoky old city from the College Wynd to St Andrew Square. He limped at full speed up and down the Cowgate in his boyhood; and 'no funeral hearse,' says Lockhart, 'crept more leisurely than did his landau in his middle age up the Canongate; not a queer tottering gable but recalled to him some long-buried memory of splendour or bloodshed, which by a few words he set before the hearer in the reality of life.'

Scott's first published work, his translations of *Lenore* and *Der Wilde Jäger* by Gottfried Burger, showed at least some talent for fluent verse, but it was during his many trips to the Borders that he greatly enlarged his knowledge of the type of verse which was going to make his reputation initially—the Border Ballads. He had long been interested in these and had collected a great number for his own amusement, and certainly without any idea of publication.

He made seven 'raids', as he called his visits, into Liddesdale where, at that time, there were no roads for carriages and he and his companion, Robert Shortreed, slept in cottages or farms that they chanced upon and enjoyed the over-generous hospitality of the area—which could involve brandy smuggled from Solway, whisky punch drunk out of milk pails and breakfasts of porter and devilled ducks.

Looking back on these expeditions, Robert Shortreed explained. 'He was makin' himsel' a' the time but he didna' ken maybe what he was about till years had passed: at first he thought o' little, I dare say, but the queerness and the fun. Eh me! Sic an endless fund o' humour and drollery as he then had wi' him! Never ten yards but we were either laughing or roaring or singing. Wherever we stopped how brawlie he suited himsel' to everybody! He ay did as the lave [rest] did; never made himsel' the great man or took any airs in the company. I've seen him in a' moods in these jaunts, grave and gay, daft and serious, sober and drunk—(this, however, even in our wildest rambles, was but rare)—but, drunk or sober, he was ay the gentleman. He looked excessively heavy and stupid when he was fou, but he was never out o' gude humour.'

It may have been an accidental meeting with James Ballantyne, an old schoolfellow, which put the idea of publication into his head. Ballantyne had left the law and was now editing and publishing the weekly *Kelso Mail*. Scott gave him some verses to print and was so pleased with the result that he suggested they should prepare a small volume of old Border ballads—to sell for four or five shillings—but as the amount of material, and his enthusiasm, grew it soon burst the bounds of a single volume. Scott's elevation to being Sheriff-deputy of Selkirkshire meant that he was close to much of the best material but he was also very fortunate in his collaborators. These included John Leyden and, later, James Hogg.

John Leyden was a self-taught prodigy who had come to Edinburgh from Roxburghshire, where his father was a shepherd, and at the age of nineteen had confounded the professors with the range and depth of his knowledge. He was very thin, with sandy hair, staring eyes and a shrill rasping voice. He looked so wild that Scott wrote, in the *Edinburgh Annual Register* of 1811, 'His first appearance was somewhat appalling to persons of low animal spirits.' One of his main interests was the Border ballads and it may have been due to his influence that the scale of the work expanded so greatly—'Dash it, does Mr Scott mean another thin thing like Goetz of Berlichingen? I have more than that in my head myself; we shall turn out three or four such volumes at least.' His scholarship, and his careful attention to the texts, about which Scott could be extremely careless, transformed the project into a major work. The book benefited most, however, from his enthusiasm about which Scott has a delightful anecdote. 'An interesting fragment had been obtained of an ancient historical ballad; but the remainder, to the great disturbance of the editor and his coadjutor, was not to be recovered. Two days afterwards, while the editor was sitting with some company after dinner, a sound was heard at a distance like that of the whistling of a tempest through the torn rigging of the vessel which scuds before it. The sounds increased as they approached more near; and Leyden (to the great astonishment of such of the guests as did not know him) burst into the room, chanting the desiderated ballad with the most enthusiastic gesture, and all the energy of what he used to call the *saw-tones* of his voice. It turned out that he had walked between forty and fifty miles and back again, for the sole purpose of visiting an old person who possessed the precious relic of antiquity.'

In 1830 Leyden left Edinburgh for India, from which he was not to return, but Scott soon found other helpers.

One of his regular correspondents was Thomas Campbell who, as he says of himself, was living in the winter of 1797 'in the Scottish metropolis by instructing pupils in Greek and Latin. In this vocation I made a comfortable livelihood as long as I was industrious. But "The Pleasures of Hope" came over me. I took long walks about Arthur's Seat, conning over my (as I thought then) magnificent lines, and as my "Pleasures of

Hope" got on, my pupils fell off.' When published, the poem took Edinburgh by storm and was praised for its sound morals, sublime conception, bold imagery, vigorous language and manly sentiment. 'Tis distance lends enchantment to the view was, reputedly, written on Calton Hill, while history records that the poem itself was written in Alison Square, which has now been destroyed. Campbell lived 'in the second floor of a stair on the north side of the central archway, with windows looking partly into the Potterrow and partly into Nicholson Street.' In 1891, when Hutton was writing, the house was still standing, although certain portions of the tenement of which it formed a part had been removed when Marshall Street had been cut through that part of the town in 1876. Another author of the period notes that 'the tenement divided Alison and Nicholson Square, but gave access to both by a pend. . . .'

Campbell and John Leyden had a petty quarrel over something and the upshot was that they refused to talk to each other. They maintained this for years and when Scott repeated the poem *Hohenlinden* to Leyden, he burst out, 'Dash it, man, tell the fellow that I hate him, but dash him, he has written the finest verses that have been published these fifty years.' Scott tried to make the peace by telling this to Campbell, who only said, 'Tell Leyden that I detest him, but I know the value of his critical approbation.'

The most noteworthy of Scott's assistants was undoubtedly James Hogg, a shepherd who had been born and lived at Ettrick. They were introduced by William Laidlaw, who was also helping in Scott's search for ballads, and with whom Scott frequently lodged. Hogg, who claimed descent from witches on his father's side and whose maternal grandfather was reputed to have been the last man in the Border to talk to the fairies, was a large raw-boned peasant with a round ruddy face and long reddish-brown hair which fell down to his waist. He was steeped in the ballad tradition and the publication of the first two volumes of the *Minstrelsy of the Scottish Border* in January 1802 had encouraged him to write down a few from his mother's recitation. She was a formidable old woman with a prodigious memory. She was highly critical of Scott's efforts. 'Ther was never ane o' my songs prentit till ye prentit them yoursel', and ye have spoilt them awthegither. They were made for singin' and no' fo readin', but ye have broken the charm now, an' they'll never be sung mair.'

Despite this outspoken criticism, Scott was delighted with his new acquaintance and invited Hogg to visit him in Edinburgh and to meet his wife, whom he described as a foreigner and dark as a blackberry. Hogg assumed that this meant she was a West Indian heiress and was much relieved when he made his way to 39 Castle Street in the following year that she was only French. This first meeting was noteworthy for other reasons, however.

When Hogg entered the drawing-room he found Mrs Scott, who was then an invalid, reclining upon a sofa. Lockhart, in his biography of Scott, writes, 'The Shepherd, after being presented and making his best bow, forthwith took possession of another sofa placed opposite to hers, and stretched himself thereupon at his full length, for, as he said afterwards, "I though I could never do wrong to copy the lady of the house". As his dress at that period was precisely that in which any ordinary herdsman attends cattle to the market, and as his hands, moreover, bore most legible marks of recent sheep-shearing, the lady did not observe the perfect equanimity the novel usage to which her chintz was exposed. The Shepherd, however, remarked nothing of all this, dined heartily and drank freely, and by jest, anecdote and song afforded plentiful merriment to the more civilized part of the company. As the liquor operated, his familiarity increased and strengthened;

90

from "Mr Scott", he advanced to "Shirra", and thence to "Scott", "Walter", and "Watty"; until at supper he fairly convulsed the whole company by addressing Mrs Scott as "Charlotte".'

The first two volumes of the *Minstrelsy* were published by Cadell and Davies, while the second edition, with the third volume, bears the imprint of Longman Hurst and Co. They were printed at Kelso by James Ballantyne, who following the success of this venture moved to Edinburgh where he soon established himself as a successful printer, partly through the large quantity of legal work obtained for him by Scott.

In the meanwhile, Scott was busy writing a poem which he hoped to include in the *Minstrelsy* but had proved to be too long. *The Lay of the Last Minstrel* had been in his mind for a considerable time, since young Lady Dalkeith of Bowhill had asked him to write a ballad on the goblin Gilpin Horner, some years before. The first canto was finished in 1802 and, in the autumn of 1803, the Wordsworths heard four of the six cantos read by the author 'in an enthusiastic kind of shout'. The poem was completed in the following year and sent off to the printers. Scott and his family were on Tweedside for New Year's Day 1805, having travelled down 'preceded by a detachment of brandy and mince pies' in case they were trapped by the snow, and in the next week *The Lay of the Last Minstrel* was published by Longman, Hurst, Rees and Orme in London, having been printed by Ballantyne.

Immediately Scott became the most popular poet of the day and edition followed edition in a manner unprecedented in the history of British poetry. Even the critics were kind, although the *Edinburgh Review,* in the person of Francis Jeffrey, complained that the poem lacked incident and that the style was parochial; 'Mr Scott must either sacrifice his Border prejudices, or offend his readers in other parts of the Empire.'

The owner of the *Review*, Archibald Constable, did not entirely agree with his editor and was quick to buy a quarter share from Longman and thus become involved in the fortunes of both Scott and Ballantyne.

Constable, born in 1774, came to Edinburgh at the age of fourteen to be an apprentice in Peter Hill's bookshop in the High Street and six years later, after marrying the daughter of a prosperous printer, he set up his own publishing house and rapidly became the head of the publishing and bookselling trade in Edinburgh. 'Abandoning the old timid, grudging system, he stood out as the general patron and payer of all promising publications; and confounded not merely his rivals in the trade, but his very authors, by his unheard of prices,' wrote Cockburn. 'Ten, even twenty, guineas a sheet for a review; £2000 or £3000 for a single poem, and £1000 each for two philosophical dissertations, drew authors from dens where they would otherwise have starved, and made Edinburgh a literary mart famous with strangers, and the pride of its own citizens.'

One of his great successes was the foundation of the *Edinburgh Review* in 1802, which marked his entrance into politics on the Whig side. The idea for the review was first propounded by the Reverend Sydney Smith to his friends, Francis Jeffrey and Henry Brougham one evening in the spring of that year at a chance meeting in Jeffrey's rooms in Buccleuch Place. At the idea of the storm such a liberal magazine would release in the predominantly Tory surroundings of Edinburgh, and England, they roared with laughter and set to work to amass material.

Smith, at the age of twenty-seven, had come to Edinburgh in 1798 to act as a private tutor. He already possessed the blandness and poise of middle age but his sound common sense was associated with an extravagant wit. He first found lodgings at

38 Hanover Street, two doors from George Street, and here on the first floor he lived for about a year. He wrote at the time, 'Our situation is in the centre of the finest street I have yet seen in Great Britain, and commands a view of the Firth shipping and the opposite shore.' But he had some domestic problems: 'The housemaid has rebelled. She has seven sweethearts and says she will go out.'

He liked the Scots, for they seemed to appreciate his wit, although he is responsible for saying, 'It requires a surgical operation to get a joke well into a Scotch understanding.' The main objection he found to Edinburgh, and Scotland, was the weather, and the Scots belief in its good qualities. 'Their temper stands anything but an attack on their climate. They would have you even believe they can ripen fruit; and, to be candid, I must own in remarkably warm summers I have tasted peaches that made most excellent pickles, and it is upon record that at the siege of Perth, on one occasion, the ammunition failing, their nectarines made admirable cannon balls. Even the enlightened mind of Jeffrey cannot shake off the illusion that myrtles flourish at Craig Crook. In vain I have represented to him that they are of the genus *carduus* [the thistle], and pointed out their peculiarities. In vain have I reminded him that I have seen hackney-coaches drawn by four horses in the winter, on account of the snow; that I had rescued a man blown flat against my door by the violence of the winds, and black in the face; that even the experienced Scotch fowls did not venture to cross the streets, but sidle along, tails aloft, without venturing to encounter the gale. Jeffrey sticks to his myrtle illusions, and treats my attacks with as much contempt as if I had been a wild visionary, who had never breathed his caller air, nor lived and suffered under the rigour of his climate.'

Smith lived in Edinburgh only until 1804—lodging first at

93

19 Queen Street and then, after his marriage, at 46 George Street—but he maintained his connections with the *Edinburgh Review* under the brilliant editorship of Francis Jeffrey.

Francis Jeffrey was the most brilliant of the young Edinburgh advocates but his sarcastic manner, the Englishness of his accent and the Whiggishness of his politics, all hindered his success. He was 'a horrid little man' but 'held in as high estimation as the Bible' and it was his puniness that had made him so sharpen his critical ability that even his friends feared it.

He was born in the four-storeyed house at 7 Charles Street and in 1801 began his married life on the third floor of 18 Buccleuch Place. It was in his little parlour here that he and Henry Brougham heard Sydney Smith's proposal for a magazine. At first Jeffrey was doubtful but he allowed himself to be overcome by Smith's enthusiasm and the wealth of talent that was available—'There was himself ready to write any number of articles,' wrote Brougham later, 'and to edit the whole; there was Jeffrey, *facile princeps* in all kinds of literature; there was myself, full of mathematics and everything relating to the colonies; there was Horner for political economy, and Murray for political subjects. Besides, might we not, from our great and never-to-be doubted success, fairly hope to receive help from such leviathans as Playfair, Dugald Stewart, Thos. Brown, Thomson and others? All this was irresistible. . . .'

Thus was born the *Edinburgh Review*, and the reception of the first issue was such as to overcome any doubts in Jeffrey's mind, or in Constable's. Later under Jeffrey's editorship, it reached the status of an institution and each issue was scanned eagerly on its arrival to see who had suffered under the scathing attacks of its reviewers or to laugh at Sydney Smith's wit. In these first years of his success Jeffrey lived at 62 Queen Street, facing the gardens, but in 1810 he moved to 92 George

Street. His last home was in an imposing mansion with tall columns at 24 Moray Place.

Carlyle, in his *Reminiscences,* says: 'I remember striding off with Proctor's introduction one evening towards George Street . . . I got ready admission into Jeffrey's study—or rather "office", for it had mostly that air—a roomy, not over-neat apartment on the ground floor, with a big baize-covered table loaded with book rows and paper bundles. On one, or perhaps two, of the walls were book shelves, likewise well filled, but with books in tattery, ill-bound, or unbound condition . . . five pairs of candles were cheerfully burning, in the light of which sat my famous little gentleman. He laid aside his work, cheerfully invited me to sit down, and began talking in a perfectly human manner.' It is to be regretted that Jeffrey never put on record his first impressions of Carlyle.

Also associated with the early days of the *Edinburgh Review* were Francis Horner, a solemn young man whom Sydney Smith described as having the 'ten commandments written on his face', and Henry Brougham, the son of an expatriate Englishman. He was born at 21 St Andrew Square, the house of the eccentric Earl of Buchan, on 19 September 1778. As a child his favourite pastime was playing at trials in which he prosecuted, defended, examined witnesses, summed up, brought in the verdict and delivered sentence. He went to a day-school in George Street when he was seven and later attended the High School, which he left as *dux* at the age of fourteen having made his mark by forcing a master to admit an error in his knowledge of Latin, and went to the University. Here he claimed to have astounded the professor of natural philosophy by deriving the Binomial Theorem unaided.

Little is known of his other places of residence in Edinburgh, although his father lived in George Street at one time and in his

Autobiography Brougham tells us only his birthplace. He does admit however, to 'high jinks'—the expression is his own—at the Apollo Club, and to oysters at Johnny Dow's (Dowie's?). He writes: 'I cannot tell how the fancy originated, but one of our constant exploits, after an evening at the Apollo or Johnny's, was to parade the streets of the New Town, and wrench the brass knockers off the doors, or tear out the brass handles of the bells. . . . It will scarcely be credited, and yet it is true as gospel, that so late as March 1803, when we gave a farewell banquet to Horner, on his leaving Edinburgh forever to settle in London, we, accompanied by the grave and most sedate Horner, sallied forth to the North Bridge, and there halted in front of Mr Manderson the druggist's shop, where I, hoisted on the shoulders of the tallest of the company, placed myself on the top of the doorway, held on by the sign, and twisted off the enormous brazen serpent which formed the explanatory announcement of the business that was carried on within.'

On another occasion, later in the same year, he instigated Professor Playfair, the Reverend Sydney Smith, and Thomas Thomson (a legal dignitary, known as jus, while his doctor brother was called pus), to attempt to filch the Galen's Head which stood over the door of Gardiner, the apothecary. By one climbing on top of the others their object was all but attained, when, by the dim light of the oil-lamps, Brougham was seen leading the city watch to the spot—a trick within a trick. All managed to escape after this action which was an early indication of the freedom from scruple and liking for independent action that marked all Brougham's later career.

Scott was also a regular contributor to the *Edinburgh Review*, at least in its early days before it became too politically committed to the Whig cause. He wrote on many topics ranging from Edmund Spenser to Colonel Thornton's Sporting Tour, and from cookery books to Ossian. But the relationship could not last. In the changing political climate the *Review* seemed to move from Whiggery to pure Jacobinism and there was a personal grudge as well. Jeffrey viewed Scott's work with high condescension and when *Marmion* appeared in February 1808 he had to send a conciliatory note to Scott with the April number, which contained a thirty-five page review of the poem. Jeffrey admitted that it had greater beauties than *The Lay of the Last Minstrel* but found its construction was loose, its diction faulty, and its narrative tedious. The review went on to caution the author: 'To write a modern romance of chivalry, seems to be much such a phantasy as to build a modern abbey or an English pagoda. For once, however, it may be excused as a pretty caprice of genius; but a second production of the same sort is entitled to less indulgence, and imposes a sort of duty to drive the author from so idle a task, by a fair exposition of the faults which are, in a manner, inseparable from its execution.'

Scott's reply was to insist that Jeffrey dine at Castle Street that night as had been arranged previously, and was as friendly as ever during the evening. Mrs Scott could not be so forgiving, however, although she contained herself throughout dinner and only burst out as Jeffrey was leaving, with 'Well, goodnight, Mr Jeffrey. They tell me you have abused Scott in the *Review*, and I hope Mr Constable has paid you very well for writing it.'

Scott's poetic star was still on the ascendant and he followed *Marmion* with *The Lady of the Lake* in 1810—a poem which marked the height of his success, for even Scott realized, after the first two cantos of *Childe Harold's Pilgrimage* had been issued in 1812, that he could not challenge Byron's genius. This was confirmed by the coolness with which *Rokeby* was received in 1813.

It was at this time that Scott 'happened to want some fishing tackle for the use of a guest', and in searching an old desk he found a long-lost manuscript of a book he had started in 1805 but laid aside because of unfavourable criticism from William Erskine. The result was, as Scott described it, the appearance of a small anonymous sort of novel in three volumes. *Waverley* was an instant success and the author was launched on his extraordinarily successful career as a novelist. Even the *Review* was kind in its criticism and Jeffrey suggested that 'if it be indeed the work of an author hitherto unknown, Mr Scott would do well to look to his laurels, and to rouse himself for a sturdier competition than any he has yet had to encounter'. Only the *Quarterly* commented unfavourably, ending its review with the wonderfully foolish comment: 'We confess that we have, speaking generally, a great objection to what may be called historical romance, in which real and fictitious person-ages, and actual and fabulous events are mixed together to the utter confusion of the reader, and the unsettling of all accurate recollections of past transactions; and we cannot but wish that the ingenious and intelligent author of *Waverley* had rather employed himself in recording *historically* the character and transactions of his countrymen *Sixty Years Since,* than in writ-ing a work, which, though it may be, in its facts, almost true, and in its delineations perfectly accurate, will yet, in sixty years *hence,* be regarded, or rather, probably, *disregarded,* as a *mere* romance, and the gratuitous invention of a facetious fancy.'

Such criticism had no effect whatsoever on sales, which soon reached three thousand, or the speculation about the author-ship. But Scott resolutely refused to reveal the secret, even going so far as to flatly deny the authorship if challenged directly by friends outside a very select circle. As he explained to his friend Morritt: 'I am something in the condition of Joseph Surface, who was embarrassed by getting himself too good a reputation; for many things may please people well enough anonymously, which, if they have me in the title-page,

William Blackwood's Office at 45 George Street

would just give me that sort of ill name which precede hanging—and that would be in many respects inconvenient if I thought of again trying a *grande opus*.' And again a fortnight later, 'I shall *not* own to *Waverley*; my chief reason is that it would prevent me of the pleasure of writing again. . . . In truth, I am not sure it would be considered quite decorous of me, as a Clerk of Session, to write novels.' He was, indeed, thinking about a second book and, in November he started *Guy Mannering* and finished writing it in six weeks. It was published in the spring of 1815, to as much acclaim as his first attempt. The first edition of two thousand copies was sold out within twenty-four hours and clearly Scott was well-established in his new career.

In the following year yet another literary light appeared for the first time. William Blackwood, a rising Edinburgh publisher of High Tory principles, decided that the time was ripe for the power of the *Edinburgh Review* to be challenged. The *Quarterly* had had little effect but Blackwood was sure that he was strong enough to challenge Constable on his own ground. The only problem was to find another Jeffrey.

His first attempt was a complete failure but he soon 'made an arrangement with a gentleman of first-rate talents by which I will begin a new work of a far superior kind'. The gentleman in question was John Wilson who, with Lockhart and Hogg, was to be largely responsible for the new *Blackwood's Edinburgh Magazine* which was to achieve fame and notoriety for its offences against literary decency.

John Wilson was described by a contemporary as looking 'like a fine Sandwich Islander who had been educated in the Highlands. His light hair, deep sea-blue eyes, tall athletic figure, and hearty hand-grasp, his eagerness in debate, his violent passions, great genius, and irregular habits, rendered him a formidable partisan, a furious enemy, and an ardent friend.' He had enjoyed a brilliant career at Oxford and was

100

the first winner of the Newdigate Prize for Poetry. His academic celebrity was surpassed by his reputation as an athlete and convivial eccentric. He moved to Edinburgh from the Lake District, after losing most of his fortune, intending to complete his studies for the bar, and lived with his mother for many years. He stayed with her even after his marriage, in 1811, at 53 Queen Street, near Castle Street, in a three-storeyed house looking out on Queen Street Gardens. In 1819 he moved to a tall and rather imposing house, 29 Anne Street, in the north-western suburbs of the city and near the Water of Leith. He went to 6 Gloucester Place in 1826, where he died in 1854.

It was at 53 Queen Street that the *Translation from an Ancient Chaldee Manuscript,* which so enraged the Edinburgh *literati* when it appeared in the first issue of Blackwood's 'maga', was concocted by Hogg, Wilson, Lockhart and even Blackwood himself. The uproarious laughter that accompanied its composition shook the walls of the house and the ladies in the room above sent to inquire in wonder what the gentlemen below were about. As a satire on the contemporary literary scene it was perhaps not in the best of taste but it shook the town with rage and mirth.

John Wilson, despite his reputation for feats of endurance and drinking, became the professor of moral philosophy in the University of Edinburgh in 1820. He knew no philosophy but he was adept at picking other people's brains. His elevation to the chair did not prevent him maintaining his reputation as an eccentric. His tall figure, clad in ancient, tattered and shapeless garments, his neck muffled with an unkempt mass of his whiskers, his blond shaggy hair covered with an old broad-brimmed hat, was familiar throughout Edinburgh. He was known to enter the lecture room surrounded by a small pack of puppies which disposed themselves around the rostrum only

101

to disturb their master's philosophical rhetoric when he trod on a protruding tail or paw.

He lived surrounded by animals and was reputed to have kept sixty-three game birds all at once. His doctor asked in wonder, 'Did they never fight?' only to be told, 'No, but put a hen amongst them, and I will not answer for the peace being long observed. And so it hath been since the beginning of the world.'

His fame today rests on his work as 'Christopher North' and, in particular, on the *Noctes Ambrosianae*. These jovial 'evenings', which consisted of a series of topical, critical, poetical and convivial dialogues, were supposed to take place in the tavern of Ambrose, in Gabriel's Road. This justly celebrated publichouse, which is said to have looked more like a farm-house on a country pathway than a city inn, has long since disappeared, and none of the local histories give it exact position. There is a strong oral tradition that it stood on the site of the New Register House, behind the old Register House, which is approached by the narrow alley running between the new Register House and the Cafe Royal.

One of the most entertaining characters in the *Noctes* and certainly one of the wildest, was the poet James Hogg, whom we have already met assisting Walter Scott with the *Minstrelsy of the Scottish Border*.

When he dropped into poetry in a professional way, Hogg came to Edinburgh, lodging in Ann Street, 'down along the North Brig towards where the new markets are, and no vera far frae the play-houses'; and sometimes he made the Harrow Inn near the Grassmarket his abiding place. Ann Street was swept out of existence altogether upon the construction of the Waverley Bridge, but an irregular row of old gabled houses, still standing, and converted into shops and tenements, from 46 to 54 Candlemaker Row, are the shells of the Harrow Inn.

102

It was in front of this tavern that Rab first introduced Dr John Brown to his friends James Noble, the Howgate carrier, and to Jess, the carrier's horse, after that Homeric dog-fight under the single arch of the South Bridge.

In 1812 and later Hogg wrote to Archibald Constable from 'Deanaugh', which was Deanhaugh Street, a row of poor-looking houses in the north-western suburbs of Edinburgh, running from Dean Terrace over the Water of Leith to Raeburn Place. Here he completed 'The Queen's Wake'.

The poor shepherd did not always approve of the behaviour attributed to him at Ambrose's tavern but he was more than pleased by the fame the association brought him. As he said, 'What is a *Noctes* without a shepherd?' He may never have achieved his ambition of being accepted as a second Burns but he was highly regarded by many sections of the community and, indeed, succeeded his more famous brother poet as poet laureate of the Kilwinning Lodge of Freemasons. Today he is best remembered for the remarkable novel *The Private Memoirs and Confessions of a Justified Sinner* which was published in 1824 but lay almost forgotten until it was taken up by André Gide.

Another of the figures who appeared at Ambrose's tavern was John Gibson Lockhart, who later achieved fame as Scott's biographer, but at this time was one of the notorious circle writing for *Blackwood's Magazine*. Born in 1794, he followed his triumphant career at Balliol by becoming an advocate in 1816, and began his dabbling in literature. He was a man of extraordinary beauty, with a well-shaped head and striking dark eyes, who carried himself like a hidalgo. He had been slightly deaf since his childhood and this accounts for the common opinion that he was shy and aloof. In the company of his friends he was known for being sympathetic and lovable and his good looks meant that there was such a demand for locks of his hair from young ladies that, in his own words, 'it threatened me with premature baldness'. It was his power of ridicule and caricature which he exploited in *Blackwood's Magazine*, however, and he was responsible for the singularly tasteless attack on Leigh Hunt. 'The extreme moral depravity of the Cockney School is another thing which is for ever thrusting itself upon the public attention, and convincing every man of sense who looks into their productions, that they who sport such sentiments can never be great poets. How could any man of high original genius ever stoop publicly, at the present day, to dip his fingers in the least of those glittering and rancid obscenities which float on the surface of Mr Hunt's Hippocrene? His poetry is that of a man who has kept company with kept-mistresses. He talks indelicately like a tea-sipping milliner girl. Some excuses for him there might have been, 'had he been hurried away by imagination or passion. But with him indecency is a disease, and he speaks unclean things from perfect inanition. The very concubine of so impure a wretch as Leigh Hunt would be to be pitied, but alas! for the wife of such a husband! For him there is no charm in simple seduction; and he gloats over it only when accompanied with adultery and incest.' Well might Walter Scott advise Lockhart to avoid anonymous, abusive journalism.

Lockhart's various dwelling places in Edinburgh from the time of his going there as a member of the Scottish bar in 1816 until his establishment in London, ten years later, are not very clearly defined. It is recorded that Scott spent much time with him one summer at his house in Melville Street, Portobello. He was at one time at 23 Maitland Street, a few doors from Athol Crescent, in 1818 and a letter of his to Hogg was addressed from 25 Northumberland Street in 1821; but in his own correspondence, and in that of his contemporaries, no hint is given as to any other of his local habitations. Naturally he was

104

often in Scott's various houses, and a guest at all of the tables of all the men of his own coterie. He died at Abbotsford, and was buried at Sir Walter's feet.

In *Peter's Letters to his Kinsfolk,* published anonymously by Lockhart in 1819—a most amusing and seemingly correct picture of the men and manners of Edinburgh at that time—he speaks with enthusiasm of the bookshop of David Laing, at 49 South Bridge. 'Here,' Lockhart says, 'my friend Wastle [Lockhart himself] commonly spends one or two hours every week he is in Edinburgh, turning over all the Aldines, Elzevirs, Wynkyn de Wordes, and Caxtons in the collection; nor does he often leave the shop without taking some little specimen of its treasures home with him.' David Laing was an accomplished antiquarian scholar, the librarian of the Signet Library, and the intimate friend of Scott, Jeffrey and their peers. As a bookseller he succeeded his father, William Laing, who had a shop in the Canongate near St Mary's Wynd.

In the autumn of 1815 Lockhart wrote to a friend describing a recent dinner party at which he had been in company with two believers in the virtues of the Lake poets—'Wilson for one, and a friend of his, a most strange creature, for the other. His name is De Quincey. . . . After dinner he set down two snuff-boxes on the table; one, I soon observed, contained opium pills—of these he swallowed one every now and then, while we drank our half-bottle apiece.'

De Quincey had not at that time published any of his thoughts—*Confessions of an English Opium Eater* was only published in 1821—but he had already so mastered the art of conversation, which he considered as an art form in itself, that many of his auditors felt his talk ranked above his later writings. One of them wrote, after meeting this diminutive scholar, 'His voice was extraordinary; it came as if from dream-land; but it was the most musical and impressive of voices. In

105

convivial life, what then seemed to me the most remarkable trait of De Quincey's character was the power he possessed of easily changing the tone of ordinary thought and conversation into that of his own dream-land, till his auditors, with wonder, found themselves moving pleasantly along with him in a sphere of which they might have heard and read, perhaps, but which had ever appeared to them inaccessible, and far, far away.'

Having successfully contributed several articles to *Blackwood's Magazine,* he decided to move to Edinburgh where he lived in Great King Street, in Forres Street and at Duddingston; later he moved to 42 Lothian Street—'in the left-hand flat on the second floor'—a house which still existed recently and was decorated with a tablet commemorating De Quincey's residence. The next tenant of these rooms, author of *Episodes of an Obscure Life,* wrote 'The good people of the house, a widow, her maiden sister, and a niece, had a very worshipful recollection of their "nice little gentleman"—that was their phrase for him. They evidently liked him, and said he was "bonnie and soft spoken".... This maiden sister seems to have been really a mature guardian angel to De Quincey. More than once she said she had "put him out", when he had fallen asleep with his head on the table, and overturned a candle on his papers. She used to buy his apparel for him piecemeal; now a pair of socks, now a pair of boots, now a coat, now a waistcoat—never a whole suit.' This last comment may explain the description of De Quincey, by another visitor, as 'a noticeably small figure, attired in a capacious garment which was made too large, and which served the purpose of both under and overcoat'.

One evening De Quincey called on Professor John Wilson in his house at 29 Ann Street, before he moved to Gloucester Place. Because it was a stormy night, the casual visitor stayed on—for nearly a year. Wilson's daughter, writing many years later of this event, said, 'An ounce of laudanum per diem prostrated animal life in the early part of the day. It was no infrequent sight to find him in his room lying on the rug in front of the fire, his head resting on a book, with his arms crossed over his breast in profound slumber. For several hours he would lie in this state until the torpor passed away; . . . the time when he was most brilliant was generally towards the early morning hours; and then more than once, in order to show him off, my father arranged his supper-parties so that sitting till 3 or 4 a.m. he brought Mr De Quincey to that point at which in charm and power of conversation he was so truly wonderful.'

De Quincey spent much of the last ten or fifteen years of his life at 'the little cottage at Lasswade' which stood on the road to Hawthornden, about a mile and a half beyond Lasswade, 'near the foot of a by-road which descends to that hollow of the Esk which contains Polton Mill and the Polton railway station'. It says much for the strength of his constitution, which he maltreated throughout his life, going so far in the period 1841 to 1844 to drink opium in large quantities much as others drank claret, that he survived to the age of seventy-three. He is buried in a grave in St Cuthbert's churchyard under a flat mural stone with a plain inscription. Let us remember him, however, as he was described by a Scottish cook, after he had ordered a simple meal, 'Weel, I never heard the like o' that in a' my days; the bodie has an awfu' sicht o' words. If it had been my ain maister that was wanting his denner he would ha' ordered a hale tablefu' in little mair than a waff o' his an', and here's a' this claver aboot a bit mutton no bigger than a preen. Mr De Quinshey would mak' a gran' preacher, though I'm thinkin' a hantle o' the folk wouldna ken what he was driving at.'

Another member of the same circle, although slightly older, was Sir Henry Raeburn, one of the greatest portrait-painters Scotland has produced. He was born at Stockbridge, a place

107

which seems to have a special affinity with artists, for David Roberts was also born there, and several artists chose to live there in the nineteenth century. As a young man he was apprenticed to a goldsmith but his talent for painting soon showed itself and after a brief period with David Martin he opened his own studio in George Street at the age of twenty.

Two years later a young lady called at the studio to have her portrait painted. As the sittings progressed Raeburn 'found that besides personal charm she had sensibility and wit. His respect for her did not affect his skill of hand, but rather inspired it. He fell in love with his sitter and made a very fine portrait of her. This lady was Countess Leslie, widow of a French count, and was so much pleased with the skill and likewise with the manners of the artist that within a month or so after . . . she gave him her hand in marriage, bestowing at once a most affectionate wife, good sense, and a handsome fortune.'

Raeburn spent the following six or seven years working in his George Street studios, earning enough to make him independent of his wife's fortune. He went to Rome in 1785, spending eighteen months there before returning to Edinburgh again in 1787, the year of Burns's visit. His talent was quickly recognized in Edinburgh and by 1795 he was at the height of his powers. This year saw his removal to the spacious studio he had built at 32 York Place, which is now converted into offices, as well as moving to the large house of St Bernard's, which stood on the ground which is now between Leslie Place and Dean Terrace. Cunningham writes, in his *Life*, 'The motions of the artist were as regular as those of a clock. He rose at seven during summer, took breakfast about eight with his wife and children, walked up to his great room in 32 York Place . . . and was ready for a sitter by nine: and of sitters he had for many years not fewer than three or four a day. To these he gave an hour and a half each. He seldom kept a sitter more

108

Raeburn's Studio at 32 York Place

than two hours unless the person happened to be gifted with more than common talents: he then felt himself happy and never failed to detain the party till the arrival of a new sitter.'

The artist used to declare that painting portraits was the most delightful occupation in the world because his sitters would arrive in the happiest of moods wearing their happiest faces, and would leave pleased to see how well they looked on canvas. A great deal of this happiness must have come from Raeburn himself, for many of his sitters have left records of how polite and gentlemanly he was, of how gay and unaffected was his manner, and of how wide-ranging were his interests. One of his sitters says, of Raeburn and his methods, 'He spoke a few words to me in his usual brief and kindly way—evidently to put me into an agreeable mood; and then having placed me in a chair on a platform at the end of his painting room, in the posture required, set up his easel beside me with the canvas ready to receive the colour. When he saw all was right, he took his palette and his brush, retreated back step by step, with his face towards me, till he was nigh the other end of his room; he stood and studied for a minute more, then came up to the canvas and without looking at me, wrought upon it with colour for some time. . . . I had sat to other artists; their way was quite different—they made an outline carefully in chalk, measured it with compasses, placed the canvas close to me, and looking me without ceasing in the face, proceeded to fill up the outline with colour . . . they gave more of the man—[Raeburn] gave most of the mind.'

The orchard of St Bernard's was a natural target for the children of Stockbridge and one day Sir Henry caught a young urchin under the trees. On being challenged the lad held up a scrap of paper on which he had been sketching the Gothic architecture of the library window. The sketch showed signs of promise and the young David Roberts was given free access to

110

the grounds and some instruction from Raeburn. Roberts was born in Stockbridge in a dilapidated house known as Duncan's Land, whose lintel bore the date 1605 and the inscription 'Fear God onlye'. As a young man he was apprenticed to a house-painter but later became a scene-painter to a travelling circus and eventually worked at Drury Lane and Covent Garden, before establishing himself as a distinguished artist. Like so many Scottish artists all his mature work was done outside Scotland.

One of David Roberts' friends was David Octavius Hill, who came to Edinburgh from Perth in the wake of his brother Alexander, who was working for Blackwood. Much of his work lay in book illustration, particularly *The Land of Burns* and the illustrated edition of the works by James Hogg. He married in 1836 and moved house to 19 Moray Place, but did not stay there long because after the death of his wife he moved his family to Inverleith Place.

The schism which occurred at the General Assembly of the Church of Scotland in 1843, and led to the establishment of the Free Church, impressed Hill who decided he would attempt to record the scene. His friend, Sir David Brewster, suggested that he use the new invention of photography (or rather 'the Calotype' as it was then called) to capture the likenesses of the more than four hundred ministers who had been present at this dramatic event. Hill decided to do this and quickly obtained portraits of all the participants, with the assistance of Dr John Adamson, one of Brewster's colleagues. This was Hill's introduction to photography and during the rest of his life he produced a truly remarkable series of photographs which are among the best dating from this period.

His painting of the disruption was eventually finished in 1866; it was a commercial failure and stands today as a monument to his industry rather than his artistry.

111

Close to Raeburn's house of St Bernard's is 21 Comely Bank, where Thomas Carlyle moved after his marriage to Jane Welsh in 1826. Francis Jeffrey was a frequent visitor here and Carlyle writes, 'he was much taken with my little Jeannie, as well he might be, one of the brightest, cleverest creatures in the whole world, full of innocent rustic simplicity and vivacity, yet with the gracefulest discernment, calmly natural deportment, instinct with beauty and intelligence to the finger ends. He became, in a sort, her would-be openly declared friend and quasi-lover; as was his way in such cases. He had much the habit of flirting about with women, especially pretty women, much more the both pretty and clever; all in a weakish, most dramatic, and wholly theoretic way (his age now fifty gone).' Comely Bank was the first home of the man and wife and in it they were as happy as it was in their power to be, meeting Wilson, De Quincey, and many other notable men and women—although never Scott—and corresponding with Goethe.

Carlyle was not quite fourteen when he first came to Edinburgh to prepare for the ministry. Accompanied by Tom Smail he set out on foot from Ecclefechan in Dumfries one cold morning in November 1809 to walk to the capital, a journey that was to take him three days. After the last stage of slightly more than twenty miles, Carlyle found his first lodging in Simon Square, in a very cheap but clean-looking house, and set out for his first view of the city which he was later to describe as an accursed, stinking, reeky mass of stones and lime and dung.

His view of the University was little different—he thought it presented a picture of the blind leading the blind—and he left in 1813 having completed the arts course but without taking a degree. He had made no headway in either classics or philosophy and the only subject in which he shone was mathematics, mainly because his talents were recognized by

Carlyle's House – 21 Comely Bank

John Leslie. He left the University to teach mathematics in his old school at Annan but neither the profession nor the place was to his liking—'the paltry trade and ditto environment for the most part were always odious to me'—and his happiest memory of this time was his friendship with Edward Irving, the founder of the Catholic Apostolic Church, better known as the Irvingites. Their first meeting in 1815, when Carlyle had come up to Edinburgh to visit Divinity Hall, was distinctly uncomfortable, for Irving badgered him with a series of questions about the domestic life of Annan. Finally, after a question about the history and condition of someone's baby, Carlyle professed total ignorance. 'You seem to know nothing,' said Irving very crossly, only to receive the choleric reply, 'Sir, by what right do you try my knowledge in this way? Are you a grand inquisitor, or have you authority to question people and cross-question at discretion? I have had no interest to inform myself about the births in Annan, and care not if the process of birth and generation there should cease and determine altogether.' Despite this poor beginning they became firm friends and Carlyle was to write 'Noble Irving! he was the faithful elder brother of my life in those years; generous, wise, beneficent, all his dealings and discoursings with me were.'

In 1817 he returned to Edinburgh to start his theological training but he already had doubts about his vocation. 'Old Ritchie was not "at home" when I called to enter myself [at Divinity Hall]. "Good," said I, "let the omen be fulfilled"' and he shook the dust of the hall from his feet for ever more.

This period saw the start of his literary career, contributing articles to an encyclopedia. He wrote, about his life in the city at this time, 'I was entirely unknown in Edinburgh circles, solitary, eating my own heart, fast losing my health too, a prey to nameless struggles and miseries, which have yet a kind of horror in them to my thoughts, three weeks without any kind of

114

sleep from impossibility to be free of noise.' By 1823 he was suffering severely from the dyspepsia that was to mark so much of his later career. One specialist whom he consulted advised him that 'It was all the tobacco, sir; give up the tobacco.' Not knowing Carlyle's strong Calvinist streak, the doctor inquired if he could give it up. 'Give it up, sir? I can cut off my hand with an axe if that should be necessary.'

After Scott's death in 1832, Edinburgh's literary eminence quickly waned as London attracted more and more men of letters—even Carlyle moving there in 1834. Scott's mantle as a historical novelist descended to Susan Ferrier, who was little more than a minor novelist, while poetry was represented by James Ballantine, the author of *The Gaberlunzie's Wallet*. One of the most endearing characters of the middle of the century was Dr John Brown, who lived in Rutland Street, surrounded by his dogs and his collection of literary relics. The author of 'Rab and his Friends', he was occasionally referred to as the 'Landseer of Literature', but this simple, kind-hearted man, a friend of Thackeray and Ruskin, produced in fact very little work.

The true successor of Ramsay, Fergusson and Scott had, however, already been born on 13 November 1850 at 8 Howard Place. Baptized as Robert Lewis Stevenson his name combined neatly the names of both his grandfathers—Robert Stevenson, who was responsible for building many of the lighthouses round the coast of Scotland, including the Bell Rock Light, and Lewis Balfour, the parish minister of Colinton. The house in Howard Place has been preserved and was for long the Stevenson Memorial and Museum.* Here gathered together was a multitude of those small personal possessions which enable us to imagine in the fullest detail the private life

* The mementoes have now been transferred to Lady Stair's House in the Lawnmarket.

of a man so well known to all through his writings. In one case lies a lock of his fair hair, cut from his head when he was four years old by his beloved nurse Cummy, while near it lies a handful of leaves and flowers from his grave in Samoa.

As a boy Robert Louis was never very strong, a weakness probably inherited from his mother, and when the family moved to 1 Inverleith Terrace in 1853 it was found that it was cold and damp and altogether unsuitable for the delicate child. So they moved again to 17 Heriot Row, a pleasant, sunny terrace facing south where the family were to live for the next thirty years. This is the house that saw the beginnings of his literary talent and it is easy to imagine the lonely, delicate child peering earnestly through the window panes, watching for 'Leerie'—'For we are very lucky, with a lamp before the door'—for it was here that many of the themes of the *Child's Garden of Verses* first stirred.

Margaret Moyes Black, who knew Stevenson as a child, wrote of him: 'He bore the burden of his bad health as bravely in those days as he did in after years, and made for himself plays and pleasures with his nimble brain while his weary body was often tired and restless in that bed whereof he had so much. His mother used to describe, with that same graphic touch which gives life to all her son wrote, the bright games the little fellow invented for himself, when he was well enough to be up and about and tell how in a corner of the room he made for himself a wonder-world all his own, in which heroes and heroines of romance loved and fought and walked and talked at the bidding of the wizard in frock and pinafore.' This description only makes it easier to believe the story of the little boy who, after a session with pencil and paper, asked, 'Mamma, I have drawed a man. Shall I draw his soul now?'

It was from this house that Stevenson went to his various schools but he was continually plagued with illness and was a

Stevenson's House – 17 Heriot Row

frequent absentee. His first school, for a very short time in 1857, was Canonmills where he was the butt of the school because of the oddity of his appearance. From this school he went to one kept in India Street by a Mr Henderson and his mother used to run him along Heriot Row in the mornings to warm him up. One of his contemporaries remembered Stevenson for the composition of the verse

> Here we suffer grief and pain
> Under Mr Hendie's cane.
> If you don't obey his laws
> He will punish with his tawse

but the attribution is extremely doubtful. Between the ages of eleven and twelve he went to the Edinburgh Academy but only infrequently, because of his health, and his main schooling took place in a school kept by a Mr Robert Thompson on the west side of Frederick Street.

His father tried to force his son into becoming an engineer, and enrolled him at the Old University on the South Bridge. The professor of Engineering was Fleeming Jenkin and the young Stevenson revelled in the 'delights of truancy' by avoiding his lectures: they were indeed the least considered item in what he called 'the vast pleasantry of his curriculum'. 'Now, Mr Stevenson,' said Jenkin, when asked for a certificate of attendance at his lectures, 'there may be doubtful cases; there is no doubt about yours. You have simply *not* attended my class.' This did not stop their personal friendship which was based on Jenkin's interest in the theatre. Stevenson was a frequent attender at the dramatic evenings held at the Jenkins' house and often played a distinguished part in the plays which the professor took very seriously.

On one occasion a Greek tragedy was presented, and after the curtain had fallen on the final scene the stage held only two of the young actors in their Greek dress. Probably as a reaction to the tragedy they threw themselves into each other's arms, executed a rapid war-dance and flung themselves on to opposite ends of a couch at the back of the stage with their feet meeting in a kind of triumphal arch in the centre. Stevenson was in command of the curtain and took one look at them before raising it rapidly. The audience gave a gasp of amazement and then broke into a roar of applause. But Professor Jenkin summoned Stevenson to his room for what he described later as 'the very worst ten minutes I ever experienced in the whole course of my life'.

After three futile years he told his father that he wanted to become a writer and was allowed to leave the engineering faculty, but only if he studied law. He succeeded in being called to the bar, and received at least four briefs—mainly through his family's influence, however—and for a long time after his departure for the South Seas, 17 Heriot Row bore a brass plate reading 'Mr R. L. Stevenson, Advocate'.

Despite this successs, his heart was no more in law than it was in engineering, and he soon devoted himself entirely to literature.

His wanderings around Edinburgh took in every part of the city but there are certain spots which will for ever be associated with him—the shop at the corner of Antigua Street immortalized in 'Penny Plain and Twopence Coloured', Greyfriars Churchyard, Calton Hill, the Dean Bridge over the Water of Leith where he doubtless dreamed of Catriona and David Balfour, and the Royal Infirmary where he met Henley.

His father's death released him from all ties with his native city, although he had spent a great deal of time away from it on account of his health. At last in 1887 he left Edinburgh for the last time, to die in distant Samoa dreaming of the 'windy parallelograms' he had so often struggled through. His actual

119

departure was recalled by one of his friends many years later. She was walking down Princes Street with a friend when 'an open cab . . . came slowly towards us, westward, along Princes Street. . . . As it passed us . . . a slender, loose-garbed figure stood up in the cab and waved a wide-brimmed hat.

'"Good-bye!" he called to us. "Good-bye!"

'"It is Louis Stevenson!" said my companion; "they must be going away again."

'The cab passed. . . . It was Edinburgh's last sight of Louis Stevenson, and Louis Stevenson's last look back at the City that was his birthplace.'

In many ways Stevenson marks the end of a tradition in Edinburgh letters and all who have succeeded him have had to forge a new literature free from the romantic influences of the past. The greatest of these in the twentieth century is undoubtedly Hugh MacDiarmid, a former student of the University, who has gathered round himself a group of writers who have revitalized Scottish letters. Novelists as diverse as Rebecca West, Mary Stewart, Muriel Spark, David Caute, and Bruce, Marshall were born or educated or lived in Edinburgh and show, in one degree or another, some signs of its influence upon them. One of her more famous adoptive residents is Sir Compton Mackenzie, who has long cast a distinguished shadow over the city of Edinburgh, which it is said has produced over six hundred poets.

Even allowing for local pride and exaggeration the 'Athens of the North' has been known by so many famous figures that it is quite obvious that they cannot all be dealt with at length in such a short study. The tradition of Scottish letters can be traced for nearly five hundred years, from before the foundation of the university and the Union of the Kingdom. In the fifteenth century Gavin Douglas had his episcopal palace in the Cowgate and William Dunbar was as familiar with the High

120

Street and its 'Stinking Style' as the palace of Holyrood. The next century saw George Buchanan living in Kennedy's Close, near the Tron Church and long since demolished, and John Knox moving from manse to manse in the High Street. Nearer modern times the number increases dramatically—not only of people living in Edinburgh but also of visitors. Defoe, who edited the Edinburgh *Courant,* stayed in 1710, while Richard Steele is reputed to have lodged in Lady Stair's Close; John Wesley preached on the Castle Hill when he was eighty-seven; Shelley, eloping unnecessarily, stayed at both 60 George Street and 36 Frederick Street; R. M. Ballantyne lived and worked in Edinburgh and Barrie was a student at the university, lodging at 3 Great King Street. The authors who were born in Edinburgh and chose to live elsewhere would make quite as impressive a list including Kenneth Grahame, who was born at 32 Castle Street, and Sir Arthur Conan Doyle, who was born at 11 Picardy Place,* but a full list of all those who, at some time, breathed the air of Auld Reekie would be too formidable to contemplate. Let us rather end with Stevenson, writing in Samoa and remembering the city: 'I was born likewise within the bounds of an earthly city illustrious for her beauty, her tragic and picturesque association, and for the credit of some of her brave sons. Writing as I do in a strange quarter of the world, and a late day of my age, I can still behold the profile of her towers and chimneys, and the long trail of her smoke against the sunset; I can still hear those strains of martial music that she goes to bed with, ending each day like an act of an opera to the notes of bugles; still recall with a grateful effort of memory, any one of a thousand beautiful and spacious circumstances that pleased me and that must have pleased any one in my half-remembered past. It is the beautiful that I thus actually recall, the august airs of the castle on its rock, nocturnal

* Regrettably demolished in 1969.

passages of lights and trees, the sudden song of the blackbird in a suburban lane, rosy and dusky winter sunsets, the uninhabited splendours of the early dawn, the building up of the city on a misty day, house upon house, spire above spire, until it was received into a sky of softly glowing clouds, and seemed to pass on and upwards by fresh grades and rises, city upon city, a New Jerusalem bodily scaling heaven.'

Blackwood's Saloon at
45 George Street as it existed
up till September 1972

The busts l. to r. represent
Professor John Wilson ('Christopher
North'), Lady Martin and Professor
William Edmonstoune Aytoun

Drawing by Dennis Flanders, A.R.W.S.

PUBLISHER'S EPILOGUE

Perhaps the final item that Sir Compton Mackenzie wrote for publication was the Foreword to this book, for he died on the last day of November 1972, as the volume was passing through the press. He was within a few weeks of his ninetieth birthday, and although not born in Edinburgh, became one of the city's most famous residents. For a number of years in the last decade of his life he had the somewhat unusual arrangement of wintering in Edinburgh, where he lived in a fine corner house at 31 Drummond Place, and spending his summers at a property he owned in the South of France.

Sir Compton wrote over one hundred books, including a multi-volume autobiography, and was a man of phenomenal memory. He was a brilliant raconteur. Members of the Independent Publishers' Guild, of which he was President, remember with affection a scintillating long address which he gave them in his eighty-eighth year.

His first novel, *The Passionate Elopement,* had been submitted (under another title) to the publisher Eveleigh Nash and rejected. Martin Secker, who was starting on his own account as a publisher, remembered this manuscript which he had read while working for Nash, and offered to include it in his own list. Thus was Mackenzie launched in 1911 and author and publisher remained firm friends ever after.

A man of independent temperament, Sir Compton was always prepared when necessary to do battle with authority and bureaucracy. He wrote a stirring book entitled *On Moral Courage,* and displayed plenty of courage in his own life.

'Sir Compton Mackenzie's burial was even attended by drama, for his body was taken to the Hebridean island of Barra (where he had lived during the 1939-45 war) by plane and an eighty-two-year-old friend who played a last lament on the bagpipes collapsed and died minutes later at the author's graveside, in a driving rainstorm.

C. S.

INDEX

Ballantyne, R.M., 121
Barrie, J.M., 121
Blacklock, Thomas, 56–7
Blackwood, William, 100, 101
Blair, Hugh, 25, 26–7, 31, 56, 64
Boswell, James, 12–18
Brougham, Henry, 92, 94, 95–6
Brown, John, 103, 115
Buchanan, George, 121
Burns, Robert, 9, 11, 28, 41, 46, 54–74

Campbell, Thomas, 88–9
Carlyle, Alexander, 25, 28, 31
Carlyle, Thomas, 95, 112–15
Caute, David, 120
Cockburn, Alicia, 76–7
Constable, Archibald, 92, 94, 100, 103
Creech, William, 37, 47, 64, 67, 71

Defoe, Daniel, 121
De Quincey, Thomas, 105–7
Douglas, Gavin, 120
Doyle, Sir Arthur Conan, 121
Drummond, William, 11–12
Dunbar, William, 120

Ferguson, Adam, 25, 28, 31, 47, 73, 75
Fergusson, Robert, 33, 47–50, 52–3, 54–5, 57, 64, 66
Flint, Sir William Russell, 42

Gay, John, 43–4
Geddes, Andrew, 42
Goldsmith, Oliver, 44
Grahame, Kenneth, 121

Hill, D.O., 111–12
Hogg, James, 80, 87, 89–91, 100, 102–3, 104, 111
Home, John, 25, 29–33
Horner, Francis, 95
Hume, David, 17–22, 25, 28, 29–30, 31, 32–3, 34
Hutton, Laurence, 9

Jeffrey, Francis, 91, 92, 94–5, 97, 98, 112
Johnson, Samuel, 12–17, 33
Jonson, Ben, 11–12

Knox, John, 121

Leyden, John, 87–8, 89
Lockhart, J.G., 33, 62–3, 73, 90, 100, 103–5

MacDiarmid, Hugh, 11, 120
Mackenzie, Sir Compton, 120, 125
Mackenzie, Henry, 28, 33–5, 46, 47, 53, 64, 65–6, 67
Marshall, Bruce, 120

Nasmyth, Alexander, 40–1
'North, Christopher , 102

Raeburn, Sir Henry, 107–10
Ramsay, Allan, the elder, 33, 35–8, 43, 53, 54, 57, 64
Ramsay, Allan, the younger, 38–40
Roberts, David, 110–11
Robertson, William, 25–6, 30

Scott, Sir Walter, 10, 11, 28, 33, 73–92, 96–100
Shelley, P.B., 121
Smith, Adam, 25, 28–9, 47
Smith, Sydney, 92–4, 96
Smollett, Tobias, 22–4, 25, 51
Spark, Muriel, 120
Steele, Richard, 121

Stevenson, R.L., 115–20, 121–2
Stewart, Dugald, 11, 44–7, 56, 64, 66, 73
Stewart, Mary, 120
Strange, Robert, 24–5

Thomson, John, 41–2

Wallace, Robert, 25
Wesley, John, 121
West, Rebecca, 120
Wilkie, David, 42–3
Wilkie, William, 25, 28
Wilson, John, 100–2, 105, 106–7